Lecture Notes in Computer Science

Vol. 49: Interactive Systems. Proceedings 1976. Edited by A. Blaser and C. Hackl. VI, 380 pages. 1976.

Vol. 50: A. C. Hartmann, A Concurrent Pascal Compiler for Mini-computers. VI, 119 pages. 1977.

Vol. 51: B. S. Garbow, Matrix Eigensystem Routines – Eispack Guide Extension. VIII, 343 pages. 1977.

Vol. 52: Automata, Languages and Programming. Fourth Colloquium, University of Turku, July 1977. Edited by A. Salomaa and M. Steinby. X, 569 pages. 1977.

Vol. 53: Mathematical Foundations of Computer Science. Proceedings 1977. Edited by J. Gruska. XII, 608 pages. 1977.

Vol. 54: Design and Implementation of Programming Languages. Proceedings 1976. Edited by J. H. Williams and D. A. Fisher. X, 496 pages. 1977.

Vol. 55: A. Gerbier, Mes premières constructions de programmes. XII, 256 pages. 1977.

Vol. 56: Fundamentals of Computation Theory. Proceedings 1977. Edited by M. Karpiński. XII, 542 pages. 1977.

Vol. 57: Portability of Numerical Software. Proceedings 1976. Edited by W. Cowell. VIII, 539 pages. 1977.

Vol. 58: M. J. O'Donnell, Computing in Systems Described by Equations. XIV, 111 pages. 1977.

Vol. 59: E. Hill, Jr., A Comparative Study of Very Large Data Bases. X, 140 pages. 1978.

Vol. 60: Operating Systems, An Advanced Course. Edited by R. Bayer, R. M. Graham, and G. Seegmüller. X, 593 pages. 1978.

Vol. 61: The Vienna Development Method: The Meta-Language. Edited by D. Bjørner and C. B. Jones. XVIII, 382 pages. 1978.

Vol. 62: Automata, Languages and Programming. Proceedings 1978. Edited by G. Ausiello and C. Böhm. VIII, 508 pages. 1978.

Vol. 63: Natural Language Communication with Computers. Edited by Leonard Bolc. VI, 292 pages. 1978.

Vol. 64: Mathematical Foundations of Computer Science. Proceedings 1978. Edited by J. Winkowski. X, 551 pages. 1978.

Vol. 65: Information Systems Methodology, Proceedings, 1978. Edited by G. Bracchi and P. C. Lockemann. XII, 696 pages. 1978.

Vol. 66: N. D. Jones and S. S. Muchnick, TEMPO: A Unified Treatment of Binding Time and Parameter Passing Concepts in Programming Languages. IX, 118 pages. 1978.

Vol. 67: Theoretical Computer Science, 4th GI Conference, Aachen, March 1979. Edited by K. Weihrauch. VII, 324 pages. 1979.

Vol. 68: D. Harel, First-Order Dynamic Logic. X, 133 pages. 1979.

Vol. 69: Program Construction. International Summer School. Edited by F. L. Bauer and M. Broy. VII, 651 pages. 1979.

Vol. 70: Semantics of Concurrent Computation. Proceedings 1979. Edited by G. Kahn. VI, 368 pages. 1979.

Vol. 71: Automata, Languages and Programming. Proceedings 1979. Edited by H. A. Maurer. IX, 684 pages. 1979.

Vol. 72: Symbolic and Algebraic Computation. Proceedings 1979. Edited by E. W. Ng. XV, 557 pages. 1979.

Vol. 73: Graph-Grammars and Their Application to Computer Science and Biology. Proceedings 1978. Edited by V. Claus, H. Ehrig and G. Rozenberg. VII, 477 pages. 1979.

Vol. 74: Mathematical Foundations of Computer Science. Proceedings 1979. Edited by J. Bečvář. IX, 580 pages. 1979.

Vol. 75: Mathematical Studies of Information Processing. Proceedings 1978. Edited by E. K. Blum, M. Paul and S. Takasu. VIII, 629 pages. 1979.

Vol. 76: Codes for Boundary-Value Problems in Ordinary Differential Equations. Proceedings 1978. Edited by B. Childs et al. VIII, 388 pages. 1979.

Vol. 77: G. V. Bochmann, Architecture of Distributed Computer Systems. VIII, 238 pages. 1979.

Vol. 78: M. Gordon, R. Milner and C. Wadsworth, Edinburgh LCF. VIII, 159 pages. 1979.

Vol. 79: Language Design and Programming Methodology. Proceedings, 1979. Edited by J. Tobias. IX, 255 pages. 1980.

Vol. 80: Pictorial Information Systems. Edited by S. K. Chang and K. S. Fu. IX, 445 pages. 1980.

Vol. 81: Data Base Techniques for Pictorial Applications. Proceedings, 1979. Edited by A. Blaser. XI, 599 pages. 1980.

Vol. 82: J. G. Sanderson, A Relational Theory of Computing. VI, 147 pages. 1980.

Vol. 83: International Symposium Programming. Proceedings, 1980. Edited by B. Robinet. VII, 341 pages. 1980.

Vol. 84: Net Theory and Applications. Proceedings, 1979. Edited by W. Brauer. XIII, 537 Seiten. 1980.

Vol. 85: Automata, Languages and Programming. Proceedings, 1980. Edited by J. de Bakker and J. van Leeuwen. VIII, 671 pages. 1980.

Vol. 86: Abstract Software Specifications. Proceedings, 1979. Edited by D. Bjørner. XIII, 567 pages. 1980

Vol. 87: 5th Conference on Automated Deduction. Proceedings, 1980. Edited by W. Bibel and R. Kowalski. VII, 385 pages. 1980.

Vol. 88: Mathematical Foundations of Computer Science 1980. Proceedings, 1980. Edited by P. Dembiński. VIII, 723 pages. 1980.

Vol. 89: Computer Aided Design - Modelling, Systems Engineering, CAD-Systems. Proceedings, 1980. Edited by J. Encarnacao. XIV, 461 pages. 1980.

Vol. 90: D. M. Sandford, Using Sophisticated Models in Resolution Theorem Proving. XI, 239 pages. 1980

Vol. 91: D. Wood, Grammar and L Forms: An Introduction. IX, 314 pages. 1980.

Vol. 92: R. Milner, A Calculus of Communication Systems. VI, 171 pages. 1980.

Vol. 93: A. Nijholt, Context-Free Grammars: Covers, Normal Forms, and Parsing. VII, 253 pages. 1980.

Vol. 94: Semantics-Directed Compiler Generation. Proceedings, 1980. Edited by N. D. Jones. V, 489 pages. 1980.

Vol. 95: Ch. D. Marlin, Coroutines. XII, 246 pages. 1980.

Vol. 96: J. L. Peterson, Computer Programs for Spelling Correction: VI, 213 pages. 1980.

Vol. 97: S. Osaki and T. Nishio, Reliability Evaluation of Some Fault-Tolerant Computer Architectures. VI, 129 pages. 1980.

Vol. 98: Towards a Formal Description of Ada. Edited by D. Bjørner and O. N. Oest. XIV, 630 pages. 1980.

Vol. 99: I. Guessarian, Algebraic Semantics. XI, 158 pages. 1981.

Vol. 100: Graphtheoretic Concepts in Computer Science. Edited by H. Noltemeier. X, 403 pages. 1981.

Vol. 101: A. Thayse, Boolean Calculus of Differences. VII, 144 pages. 1981.

Vol. 102: J. H. Davenport, On the Integration of Algebraic Functions. 1–197 pages. 1981.

Vol. 103: H. Ledgard, A. Singer, J. Whiteside, Directions in Human Factors of Interactive Systems. VI, 190 pages. 1981.

Vol. 104: Theoretical Computer Science. Ed. by P. Deussen. VII, 261 pages. 1981.

Vol. 105: B. W. Lampson, M. Paul, H. J. Siegert, Distributed Systems – Architecture and Implementation. XIII, 510 pages. 1981.

Vol. 106: The Programming Language Ada. Reference Manual. X, 243 pages. 1981.

Lecture Notes in Computer Science

Edited by G. Goos and J. Hartmanis

150

Enduser Systems and Their Human Factors

Proceedings of the Scientific Symposium conducted
on the occasion of the 15th Anniversary of the
Science Center Heidelberg of IBM Germany
Heidelberg, March 18, 1983

Edited by A. Blaser and M. Zoeppritz

Springer-Verlag
Berlin Heidelberg GmbH

CR Subject Classifications (1982): H 1.2

ISBN 978-3-540-12273-9   ISBN 978-3-540-39588-1 (eBook)
DOI 10.1007/978-3-540-39588-1

2145/3140-543210

CONTENTS

Introduction   1
A. BLASER, M. ZOEPPRITZ

KEYNOTE ADDRESS

Human Factors of Interactive Software   9
B. SHNEIDERMAN

ENDUSER SYSTEMS

The Integrated Data Analysis and Management System -
A Generator for Enduser Systems   30
U. SCHAUER

Human Factors of a "Natural Language" Enduser System   62
M. ZOEPPRITZ

VARIOUS ASPECTS OF THE HUMAN FACTORS PROBLEM

Analytic Tools for Human Factors of Software   94
P. REISNER

Human Factors Aspects in Organizations
and Information Systems Supporting Them   122
F. KRÜCKEBERG

The Contribution of Artificial Intelligence
to the Human Factors of Application Software   128
W. v. HAHN

INTRODUCTION

The last decade has seen a wealth of research about enduser oriented
software systems for interactive, "creative" use, e.g. for text processing, problem solving / decision making, and application development. Very high level query languages on the basis of data base
management systems are just one example. Implementation has become
possible and feasible through the steadily increasing power of
computing systems at decreasing cost.

Many proposals and prototypical implementations of enduser systems
and their user interfaces originated from the imagination and common
sense of researchers and designers largely without recourse to the
knowledge and advances in cognitive psychology. They reflect what
the computer scientists - not the endusers - thought might be easy to
use and useful for users not trained in data processing. Again,
developments in high level query languages are an example: A multi-
tude of (sometimes only slightly) different data base query languages
were invented since E.F. Codd wrote his first landmark paper on relational data bases. In a survey in 1979 we have reviewed some 40
research proposals, whose authors often claimed, that their particular language was "better" than others with respect to
userfriendliness, ease of use, ease and speed of learning, ease of
memorization, etc., but there was little testing of their claims.

In the early 70's some researchers - mostly in the USA - started to
approach the question of "userfriendliness of software", initially
using research techniques which were to some extent analogous to
those used in research about hardware ergonomics. At this time, the
notion of human factors (ergonomics) had its tradition in the study
of the effects of hardware machinery on man. To study these effects,
experimentation and physiological measurements were mainly used. With
the quickly and vastly spreading on-line use of computers for
shop-floor and clerical office tasks, and with the growing concern
for humanization of labour, the computer-related ergonomics research
concentrated on the userfriendliness of I/O devices such as CRT
screens, special purpose terminals, keyboards, printers, etc. Here
the research problems were better defined and the results led to
significantly improved hardware.

Research on human factors of software began to establish itself using experimental methods derived both from hardware ergonomics and from experimental psychology. On an organizational level, surveys were conducted to identify problem areas. There were results. Textbooks about human factors of software and programmer psychology were written. Now, guidelines and checklists are offered to software developers to help them make usable software. The suggestions offered there range from the obvious - but ever achievable? - request for a detailed and complete description of the eventual users of the system, to details like rules for screen lay-out and the number of items in a menu. We believe that the most important result of this activity is a general awareness of the software human factors issue (the fact that the Human Factors Conference at Gaithersburg, Maryland, in March 1982 had over 900 attendees and that IFIP'83 has invited a paper on "Ease of Use - A System Design Challenge", can be taken in evidence).

Nevertheless, the question of what makes an application system really "easy to use" is wide open. There are many small results, but we are far from having a yardstick and a measurement technique with which we can judge a specific system design with respect to the system's usability in different modes of usage (e.g. learning vs. routine use). Even if perfect requirements and a complete, detailed description of the eventual users of a system were given, and even if simulation techniques and testing with representatives of the users were applied, it still seems to be nearly impossible to compare alternative designs and to judge which one is "best" in terms of its human factors without observing the respective systems in real use - an economically infeasible proposition. In brief: We lack the prerequisites for systematic construction of systems with good human factors, on schedule, and at reasonable cost (bad timing and unaffordable cost are bad human factors).

This unsatisfactory situation is particularly felt by those, who have been claiming in the past to develop enduser oriented, userfriendly systems, interfaces, languages, etc. To them it seems rather obvious that continuing to invent and develop new systems with only supposedly better user interfaces is not the systematic way to fundamentally improve the situation. It seems more promising to work towards a better understanding of the notion of userfriendliness by using the techniques of human factors research in order to study the large number of systems available - at least as prototypes - today.

This was one of the reasons why IBM Germany included the subject area "Human Factors of Application Software" in the research programme of its Heidelberg Science Center, after this center had been involved in enduser systems research for nearly a decade. In selecting "Enduser Systems and their Human Factors" as the topic of the scientific symposium conducted to celebrate its 15th anniversary, the center wanted to emphasize research which is as much related to its past as to its future.

The symposium had two objectives: First, it intended to exemplify some of what is known about enduser systems in the context of the usability issue (using examples from the center's past research) and to summarize the knowledge about the human factors of such systems and about the proper research methods. Secondly, it aimed at pointing to important open questions and to the future potential for finding the respective answers. We do hope that these objectives have been met as far as this is possible at all in one day.

The structure of the symposium was straight forward. After a keynote address by Prof. Dr. B. Shneiderman, University of Maryland, two contributions by U. Schauer and M. Zoeppritz, Heidelberg Science Center, were devoted to the past enduser systems research of this center, and three subsequent papers by Dr. P. Reisner, IBM Research San Jose, Prof. Dr. F. Krückeberg, GMD Birlinghoven, and Prof. Dr. W. v. Hahn, University of Hamburg, addressed various aspects of the human factors problem.

All the contributions have been invited. Nevertheless, the contents of the introduction and of the papers express the authors' own, personal opinions and not IBM's.

The keynote paper by Prof. Dr. B. Shneiderman, University of Maryland, entitled Human Factors of Interactive Software relates the high interest in the subject area to the spreading use of computers for life-critical applications, in industrial/commercial/office environments, and at home, each situation posing its own particular human factors requirements. The paper gives suggestions for system designers and developers to help them assure good human factors of their system which might be decisive for its success in a highly competitive market. They have to set for themselves measurable human factors design goals, such as time to learn, speed of performance, rate of errors, etc., in addition to such primary design goals as proper functionality, adequate reliability, and suitable cost. Shneiderman emphasizes that the corresponding human factors acceptance tests, like any other test, have to be planned early in the development process and properly conducted before shipment of the system. The paper also lists some sources of information about the human factors issue. Resorting to them for help is essential, but still cannot substitute for the involvement of users in the development process. The author complements this very practical part of his paper by a list of potential research projects he recommends to be undertaken. Problems such as response time / display rates vs. operator productivity, menu selection and structure, command languages, graceful evolution of novice to experienced users, online assistance, programming style, documentation, etc., are on this list. Prof. Shneiderman concludes - as he concluded many years ago for his own research - that this rich set of promising research problems should be addressed by academia and industry, doing experimentation and applying psychology, in order to improve our basic knowledge and the set of tools and guidelines for system developers, and in order to raise the consciousness of the general public.

The Integrated Data Analysis and Management System (IDAMS), a research prototype of an enduser systems generator developed over the past seven years at the Heidelberg Science Center, is presented by U. Schauer in the second paper. Emphasis is put on those issues of system and interface design which were derived from the principles that the research team applied regarding usability (two-dimensional, display oriented, high level language with a minimum of language rules; consistency and principle of least surprise; extensibility & adaptivity; menu or command driven dialogs at the user's discretion; user guidance; user profiles; permanent and active dictionary; recovery from error situations; etc.). These issues are complicated by the fact that the system was to be application independent, and that it was to support application development processes (partly to be done by the enduser himself) leading to application specific decision support systems. One of the conclusions drawn from usability studies is that the functional richness and power of a system is in serious conflict with what people usually perceive as userfriendly. Using the system in its entirety for solving a problem might be difficult, although each individual step in the man/machine interaction is system supported and easy. It is not certain whether profiling can remedy this situation.

The User Specialty Languages System (USL) of the Heidelberg Science Center is a research prototype of an enduser oriented question/answer system which allows users to interrogate relational data bases in restricted natural language (English, German, Spanish) from CRT or typewriter terminals. Here too, the system is application independent. Application development is done by structuring a particular relational data base and by introducing the respective application specific terms into the language interface (the latter can be done by the enduser himself). While IDAMS applied a number of userfriendliness concepts, USL's good human factors was to be its language. The paper of M. Zoeppritz briefly introduces the USL system. Its main emphasis, however, is to comment on some of the arguments offered for and against natural language for data base manipulation and - more general - for man/machine interaction. This is done on the basis of data and observations collected from the use of USL in real applications. The studies showed that restricted natural language systems are feasible today and that people can work with them, although they behave quite differently from natural language dialogues between human beings. The paper concludes that having natural language does, of course, not preclude the necessity for proper diagnostics, good menues, clear manuals, etc., but that there are features of natural language that make it desirable from a human factors point of view. Users use natural language with greater confidence in their ability to express what they mean and they learn to cope with the restrictions of the system in the spirit of those who know better. Users did not seem to expect the machine to act like a human being. They were fully aware of the fact that their partner in the dialogue was a strict machine, insensible but logical and reliable, i.e not an "intelligent" human being.

Human factors studies generally rely on behavioural experiments. Such experiments can have many purposes, such as research, system design, quality control, or making a decision whether to purchase or market a system. Whatever the purpose, such experiments have one thing in common: they are usually difficult , time consuming, and expensive. Furthermore, a running system - or at least a prototype of one - is usually required, or it has to be simulated. In system development, this has the effect that the results may just come too late in the development cycle to be useful for design decisions. The paper of Dr. P. Reisner, IBM Research San Jose, on "Analytic Tools for Research in Human Factors of Software" discusses studies which take - for the above reasons - a non-experimental, analytic approach to the problem. They aim at an abstract representation of relevant elements of a particular system that can be manipulated to predict ease of use. Thus, the central concept is the notion of "prediction", not "after-the-fact-testing". The analytic tools themselves need to be validated to determine whether what they predict about ease of use is really true. Such validation generally takes the form of behavioural experiments but what they test are the tools rather than particular systems. As examples of such research, Card's Keystroke Level Model, Moran's Command Grammar, and Reisner's Action Language are discussed. The latter research suggests the formal description of the syntax and semantics of the man/machine interface in question using Backus-Naur notation. It tries to prove that one can identify complicated concepts of an interface from its formal description. The paper describes the basic concepts and ongoing research in the area and concludes that the work described may at this time not represent more than a trend of analytic tools and that it is difficult as yet to see a clear substructure within it, since it is sparse and does not consistently encompass all three elements desired for an analytic tool (abstract representation, manipulation, validation). But it seems at least possible in principle to include all three and there is a good chance for success. Thus, a technique seems to be in sight which might one day make it possible to decide on what is easy or complicated in an interface prior to its implementation.

The paper of Prof. Dr. F. Krückeberg, GMD Birlinghoven on "Human Factor Aspects in Organizations and Information Systems Supporting Them" goes beyond the human factors of software to look at ergonomics in a wider sense. Given the basic meaning of ergonomics as "adjusting the working conditions of people to their capabilities", this encompasses people's tasks within organizations, their relationships and communication with one another as well as hardware, software, and communication systems. The paper distinguishes three interrelated levels of human capability: organic functions, cognitive capabilities, and the ability to provide meaning. These levels are then related to three aspects of ergonomics, i.e. technical (hardware) ergonomics, communications (software) ergonomics, and organizational ergonomics. The paper elaborates on the informational, technological and organizational consequences of this three-level structure and shows constructive ways for the introduction of human factors consid- erations into information systems and organizations. The paper concludes that future information systems technology must emphasize organizational ergonomics in addition to hardware and software ergo- nomics. To mention just one obvious example: Demands for face-to-face communication and for integrated, cooperative work procedures both have to be satisfied by the design options chosen. In consequence, it is not sufficient to assess the human factors of particular system aspects in isolation. Whatever results research can achieve on indi- vidual aspects, researchers and system designers have to view these results in the context of people's overall work situation and organ- izational environment. It is now essential that this proposal can soon be substantiated and transformed into practical guidelines.

In the last paper of this symposium, Prof. Dr. W. v. Hahn, University of Hamburg, deals with the interesting question of the potential "Contribution of Artificial Intelligence to the Human Factors of Application Software". The subject was chosen due to the extreme controversies artificial intelligence raises in the discussion about the ease of use of computers, ranging from "there is no userfriendli- ness at all without AI" to "AI will never live up to its promises". Since the author is involved in natural language research, his paper mainly deals with speech recognition and natural language processing, i.e. written or spoken natural language communication with computers, but it is by no means restricted to it. It also addresses some mechanical, cognitive and social aspects of ergonomics in such fields of artificial intelligence as vision, robotics, and theorem proving. A few of their benefits now visible are emphasized. The author concludes that, in order to assess the value of natural language AI-systems, research must consider the natural (language) environment of the problem solving process with its heterogeneous types of infor- mation and it must accept highly restricted language utterances as linguistically appropriate for specific task environments. In his opinion, natural language systems will only become beneficial if their cognitive and communicative abilities dominate rather than their linguistic ones, if they realize an elementary dynamic partner model, and if an explanation component makes them transparent for their users.

"Human performance in the use of computers and information systems will be a rapidly expanding research topic in the next decades". We hope that this symposium is already evidence that this prediction of Prof. Shneiderman's is beginning to come true or that it stimulates research to help make it become true. To loosely quote him further: "The opportunities for researchers are unlimited. There are so many interesting, important, and doable projects, that it may be hard for someone to choose a direction. If it is done and a research project is selected, one should begin by understanding the practical background of it, consider the fundamental psychological principles of human behaviour, and propose a lucid, testable hypothesis. Then one should consider the appropriate research methodology, collect the data, and analyze the results. But one should not stop here. It is essential to return finally to the practical application area with specific recommendations, and to refine one's model of human performance". What a challenge!

The symposium was organized by the IBM Science Center at Heidelberg and sponsored by IBM Germany. The editors would like to express their gratitude and appreciation to the sponsor, to all lecturers, to the many contributors within and outside of IBM who gave advice and assistance in preparing, organizing and running this symposium, in particular to Prof. Dr. R. Hartwig, the local organizer, and to other colleagues at the Heidelberg Science Center, and last but not least to the Springer Publishing Company for producing the proceedings in the usual outstanding quality and under the obviously unavoidable time pressure.

Heidelberg, January 1983

    M. Zoeppritz   A. Blaser

HUMAN FACTORS OF INTERACTIVE SOFTWARE

Ben Shneiderman
University of Maryland
College Park, MD 20742 USA

Abstract: There is intense interest about human factors issues in
interactive computer systems for life-critical applications, indus-
trial/commercial uses, and personal computing in the office or home.
Primary design goals include proper functionality, adequate reliability, suitable cost, and adherence to schedule. Measurable human
factors issues include time to learn, speed of performance, rate of
errors, subjective satisfaction, and retention over time. Specific
human factors acceptance tests are described as a natural complement
to hardware and software acceptance tests. Project management ideas,
information resources, and potential research directions are
presented.

1. INTRODUCTION

Civilization is a product of the tools and processes created to serve
people. Neolithic stone tools for hunting and construction, Medieval
weapons and armor, Gutenberg's movable type for printing, Daguerre's
photographic processes, the automobile, and television are but a few
of the dramatic inventions which have shaped the evolution of
history. The first products were crude, but each technology was eventually refined to accommodate human needs.

New technologies are often difficult to use, but provide remarkable,
almost supernatural, powers to those who master them. Then the technology becomes more reliable and widely used. Eventually it becomes
integrated into common experience, so that its absence is a severe
loss.

Computer systems are a new technology in the first stages of refinement and dissemination. The opportunities for designers and entrepre-
neurs are substantial, but only a fraction of the potential usage has
been explored. Like early photography or automobiles, computers are
available only to those who devote extensive effort in mastering the

technology. Harnessing the computer's power is a task for designers who understand the technology and are sensitive to human capacities and needs.

Human performance in the use of computer and information systems will be a rapidly expanding research topic in the next decades. This interdisciplinary topic combines the experimental methods and intellectual framework of cognitive psychology with the powerful and widely used tools developed from computer science.

Closely related fields include education where computers are increasingly used in programs ranging from elementary school through professional skills development. The theory and measurement techniques of educational psychology are applicable to studying the learning process in novice computer users. Business system design and management decision making are endeavors which are being increasingly shaped by the nature of the computer facilities. Library and information services are also dramatically influenced by the availability of computer-based systems.

In these disciplines and certainly others, there is growing interest in the human factors issues of computer use with systems such as:

- text editors
- electronic mail and computer conferencing
- videotext/viewdata
- programming environments and tools
- bibliographic retrieval
- information and database search
- personal and home computing
- computer-based education
- commercial systems such as inventory, personnel, and reservations
- decision support systems
- electric utility and air traffic control
- entertainment.

Design issues include novice vs. expert differences, command language vs. menu selection, graphical approaches, speech input and output, response time and display rates, novel input and output devices, keyboard design, on-line assistance, tutorials, and consultants,

documentation, training, evaluation methods, experimental techniques,
cognitive models of user behavior, organizational impact, and social
issues.

2. PRIMARY DESIGN GOALS

Every interactive system designer wants to build a high quality
system that is admired by colleagues, celebrated by users, circulated
widely, and frequently imitated. Appreciation comes, not from flam-
boyant promises or stylish advertising brochures, but from inherent
quality features which are arrived at by thoughtful planning, a
sensitivity to user needs, careful attention to detail in design and
development, and diligent testing. Multiple design alternatives are
raised for consideration and the leading contenders subjected to
further development and testing. Evaluation of designs refines the
understanding of appropriateness for each choice.

Successful designers go beyond the vague notion of "user
friendliness" and probe deeper than a checklist of subjective guidelines. They must have a thorough understanding of the diverse community of users and the tasks that must be accomplished. The first
step is to ascertain the necessary functionality - what tasks and
subtasks must be carried out. The frequent tasks are easy to determine, but the occasional tasks, the exceptional tasks for emergency
conditions, and the repair tasks to cope with errors in use of the
system are more difficult to discover. Task analysis is central,
because systems with inadequate functionality frustrate the user and
are often rejected or underutilized. If the functionality is inadequate it doesn't matter how well the human interface is designed.
Excessive functionality is also a danger, and probably the more
common mistake of designers, because the clutter and complexity make
implementation, maintenance, learning, and usage more difficult.

The second step is ensuring proper system reliability. The software
architecture and hardware support must ensure high availability, ease
of maintenance, and correct performance. If the system is not func-
tioning or introduces errors, then it doesn't matter how well the
human interface is designed. Attention must also be paid to ensuring
privacy, security, and information integrity. Protection must be

provided from unwarranted access, inadvertent destruction of data, or malicious tampering.

The third step is to plan carefully to be on schedule and within budget. Delayed delivery or cost overruns can threaten a system because the confrontive political atmosphere in a company or the competitive market environment contain potentially overwhelming forces. If an in-house system is late then other projects are effected and the disruption may cause managers to choose an alternative. If a commercial system is too costly, customer resistance may emerge to prevent widespread acceptance which allows competitors to capture the market.

When these three steps - identifying adequate functionality, ensuring system reliability, and scheduling and budgeting - are taken care of, the human factors aspects of the design can be considered.

3. HUMAN FACTORS DESIGN GOALS

If adequate functionality has been chosen, reliability is ensured, and schedule plus budgetary planning is complete, then attention can be focussed on the human factors issues. The multiple design alternatives must be evaluated for specific user communities and for specific benchmark sets of tasks. A clever design for one community of users may be inappropriate for another community. An efficient design for one class of tasks may be inefficient for another class.

The Library of Congress Experience

The relativity of design played a central role in the evolution of information services at the Library of Congress. Two of the major uses of computer systems were for cataloging new books and for searching the on-line book catalog. Separate systems for these tasks were created which optimized the design for one task and made the complementary task difficult. It would be impossible to say which was better, because they were both fine systems, but serving different needs. It would be like asking whether the New York Philharmonic Orchestra was better than the New York Yankees baseball team.

The bibliographic search system, SCORPIO, was very successfully used by the staffs of the Library of Congress, the Congressional Research Service (CRS), and the Senate and House of Representatives. They could do bibliographic searching, and used the same system to locate and read CRS reports, to view events recorded in the bill status system, and much more. The professional staff members took a three to six hour training course and then could use terminals in their office where more experienced colleagues could help out with the problems and where adequate consultants were usually available.

Then in January 1981, the Library of Congress stopped entering new book information in the card catalogs, thus requiring the general public to use one of the eighteen terminals in the main reading room to locate the new books. For even a computer/knowledgeable individual, learning to use the commands, understanding the cataloging rules, and formulating a search strategy would be a challenging task. The reference librarians claimed that they could teach a willing adult the basic features in fifteen minutes, but fifteen minutes per patron would overwhelm the staff and more importantly, most people are not interested in investing even fifteen minutes in learning to use a computer system. The library patron has work to do and often perceives the computer as an intrusion or interference with their work. The SCORPIO system which worked so well for one community of users, was improperly designed for this new community.

The system designers revised the on-line messages to provide more supportive and constructive feedback, offered extensive on-line tutorial material, and began to explore the use of menu selection approaches for the novice users. In short, a new community of users demanded substantial redesign of the human interface.

Measurable human factors issues

Once a determination has been made of the user community and the benchmark set of tasks, then the human factors issues can be examined. Again and again I returned to these five measurable human factors issues:

- time to learn. How long does it take for typical members of the target community to learn how to use the task relevant set of commands.

- <u>speed of performance.</u> How long does it take to carry out the benchmark set of task?
- <u>rate of errors.</u> How many and what kind of errors are made in carrying out the benchmark set of tasks? Although time to make and correct errors might be incorporated into the speed of performance, error making is such a critical component of system usage that it deserves extensive study.
- <u>subjective satisfaction.</u> How well did users like using aspects of the system? This can be ascertained by interview or written surveys which include satisfaction scales and space for free form comments.
- <u>retention over time.</u> How well do users maintain their know-ledge after an hour, day, or week? Retention may be closely linked to ease of learning, frequency of use plays an important role.

Every designer would like to succeed in every issue, but there are often forced trade-offs. If lengthy learning is permitted, then task performance speed may be reduced. If rate of errors is to be kept extremely low, then speed of performance may have to be sacrificed. In some applications, subjective satisfaction may be the key determi-nant of success, while in others short learning times or rapid performance may be paramount. Project managers and designers must be aware of the trade-offs and make their choices explicit and public. Requirements documents and marketing brochures should make clear which issues are primary.

4. HUMAN FACTORS ACCEPTANCE TEST

Once the decision about the relative importance of each of the human factors issues has been made, specific measurable objective should be established to guide designers and implementers. The acceptance test plan for a system should be included in the requirements document and should be written before the design is made. Hardware and software test plans are regularly included in requirements documents; extend-ing the principle to human interface development is natural.

The requirements document for a word processing system might include this acceptance test:

The subjects will be 35 secretaries hired from an employment agency with no word processing experience, but typing skills in the 35-50 words per minute range. They will be given 45 minutes of training on the basic features. Then at least 30 of the 35 secretaries should be able to complete 80 percent of the typing and editing tasks in the enclosed benchmark test correctly within 30 minutes.

Another testable requirement for the same system might be:

After four half days of regular use of the system, 25 out of these 35 secretaries should be able to carry out the advanced editing tasks in the second benchmark test within 20 minutes while making fewer than 6 errors.

This second acceptance test captures performance after regular use. The choice of the benchmark tests is critical and highly system dependent. The test materials and procedures must also be refined by pilot testing prior to use.

A third item in the acceptance test plan might focus on retention:

After two weeks, at least 15 of the test subjects should be recalled and be required to perform the third benchmark test. In 40 minutes at least 10 of the subjects must be able to complete 75 percent of the tasks correctly.

Such performance tests constitute the definition of "user friendly" for this system. By having an explicit definition, both the managers and the designers will have a clearer understanding of the system goals and whether they have succeeded. The presence of a precise acceptance test plan will force greater attention to human factors issues during the design and ensure that pilot studies are run to determine if the project can meet the test plan goals.

In a programming workstation project, the early requirement for performance helped shape the nature of the interface. That require-ment was:

New professional programmer users should be able to sign on, create a short program, and execute it against a stored test data set, without assistance and within 10 minutes.

Specific goals in acceptance tests are useful, but competent test managers will notice and record anecdotal evidence, suggestions from participants, subjective reactions of displeasure or satisfaction, their own comments, and exceptional performance (both good and bad) by individuals. The precision of the acceptance test provides an environment in which unexpected events are most noticeable.

5. MOTIVATIONS FOR HUMAN FACTORS IN DESIGN

The enormous interest in human factors of interactive systems arises from the complementary recognition of how poorly designed many current systems are and from the genuine desire to create elegant systems which effectively serve the users. This increased concern emanates from three primary sources: life-critical systems, industrial/commercial uses, and office, home, and entertainment applications.

Life-critical systems

Life-critical systems include air traffic, nuclear reactor, or power utility control, medical intensive care or surgery, manned spacecraft, police or fire dispatch, and military operations. In these applications high costs are expected, but they should yield high reliability. Lengthy training periods may be acceptable to obtain rapid, error free performance. Subjective satisfaction is less of an issue and retention is obtained by frequent use.

Industrial/commercial uses

Typical industrial/commercial uses include banking, insurance, order entry, inventory management, airline, hotel, or car rental, utility billing, credit card management, and point-of-sales terminals. In these cases, costs shape many judgments; lower cost may be preferred even if there is some sacrifice in reliability. Operator training time is expensive, so ease of learning is important. The trade-offs for speed of performance and error rates are decided by the total cost over the system lifetime. Subjective satisfaction is of modest importance and again retention is obtained by frequent use. Speed of performance becomes central for most of these applications because of the high volume of transactions. Trimming ten percent off of the mean transaction time means ten percent fewer operators, ten percent fewer terminal workstations, and possibly a ten percent reduction in hardware costs. A 1982 study by a leading motel chain reported that a one second reduction in the 150 second mean time per reservation would save $ 40,000 per year.

Office, home, and entertainment applications

The rapid expansion of office, home, and entertainment applications is the third source of interest in human factors. Personal computing applications include word processing, customer bank terminals, video games, educational packages, information retrieval, electronic mail, computer conferencing, and small business management. For these systems ease of learning, low error rates, and subjective satisfaction are paramount because use is frequently discretionary and competition is fierce. If the users can't succeed quickly they will abandon the use of a computer or try a competing package. In cases where use is intermittent, retention is important, so on-line assistance becomes very important.

Choosing the right functionality is difficult; novices are best served by a constrained simple set of actions, but as experience increases so does the desire for more functionality. Layered or level structured designs are one approach to graceful evolution from novice to expert usage. As users gain competence, their desire for more rapid performance and extensive functionality grows. Low cost is important because of lively competition, but extensive design and testing can be amortized over the large number of users.

These three stereotypical classes leave out many applications, but a similar analysis of needs can be performed. The first step in design is to make explicit the goals and metrics of success.

6. MANAGING THE DESIGN PROCESS

In the first decades of computer software development, senior programmers designed text editors, operating system control languages, programming languages, and applications packages for themselves and their peers. Now the user population for office automation, home and personal computing, and point of sales terminals is so vastly different, that the experience and intuition of senior programmers may be inappropriate. Designs must be validated through pilot and acceptance tests which can also provide a finer understanding of user skills and capabilities.

The egocentric style of the past must yield to humility and a genuine desire to accommodate to the user's skills, wishes, and orientation. Designers must seek more direct interaction with the users during the design phase, development process, and throughout the system lifecycle. Corporate marketing departments are aware of these issues and are a source of constructive encouragement. When more than two hundred suppliers provide similar word processing packages, human engineering is vital for product acceptance.

While many organizations maintain a human factors group which is a source of experience and expertise in testing techniques, in some cases, this resource is not used because the group members are not familiar with the application area, are perceived as being outsiders, or must be paid as if they were external consultants. Development projects might be better served if a human factors role were assigned to a team member, or to several members if the project is large. The human factors coordinator for a project would develop the necessary skills for the project and would be more effective in communicating with external human factors professionals when further expertise, references to the literature, or experimental tests were required. This dual strategy balances the needs for centralized expertise and decentralized application. It enables professional growth in the human factors area and in the application domain.

As projects grow in complexity, size, and importance role specialization will emerge, as it has in architectural, aircraft, or book design. Eventually individuals will become highly skilled in specific problems such as dialog management techniques, graphic display algorithms, voice and audio tone design, writing of messages and menus, or on-line tutorial writing. Consultation with graphic artists, book designers, advertising copy writers, instructional text book authors, or movie animation creators may be useful. Perceptive system developers will recognize and employ psychologists for experimental testing, sociologists for evaluating organizational impact, educational psychologists for refining training procedures, and psychiatric social workers for guiding user consultants or customer service personnel.

7. INFORMATION RESOURCES

There is an enormous volume of literature in computer science, psychology, human factors, and other areas which might be relevant, but some sources are especially rich. Two prominent journals which focus on questions of human performance with computers are:

Behavior and Information Technology

International Journal of Man-Machine Studies

Other journals regularly carry articles of interest:

ACM Computing Surveys

Communications of the ACM

Ergonomics

Human Factors

IBM Systems Journal

IEEE Computer

IEEE Transactions on Systems, Man, and Cybernetics

Journal of Applied Psychology.

The Association for Computing Machinery (ACM) has a Special Interest Group on Computer & Human Interaction (SIGCHI) which publishes a quarterly newsletter and holds regularly scheduled conferences. The American Society for Information Science (ASIS) has a Special Interest Group on User On-line Interaction (SIGUOI) which publishes a quarterly newsletter and participates by organizing sessions at the annual ASIS convention. The International Federation for Information Processing has a working group WG 6.3 on human computer interaction which publishes a quarterly newsletter called Interact.   The Human

Factors Society has a Computer Systems Group with a quarterly news-letter, as well.

Conferences, such as the ones held by the ACM, ASIS, National Computer Conference Board of AFIPS, Human Factors Society, and IFIP often have relevant papers presented and published in the proceedings. The list of guidelines documents, books, and articles may be seen as a starting point to the large and growing literature in this area.

8. POTENTIAL RESEARCH PROJECTS

There are so many fruitful directions for research that any list can only be a provocative starting point. These topics indicate my thoughts about where effort could and should be applied:

1) Response time, display rates, and operator productivity - many computer professionals believe in the simple principle that faster is always better. There is evidence from several IBM studies and other sources that programmers are more productive when system response time is kept within the one second range or even faster. On the other hand isolated studies have shown that in some business decision making tasks, computer assisted instruction, complex order entry, and introductory sessions with novices rapid performance leads to poorer learning, less effective decisions, higher error rates, and occasionally decreased satisfaction. A thorough study of multiple tasks with a variety of user communities would shed light on which situations would be improved with shorter response times or faster display rates. Understanding psychological issues of short-term memory load, decision making strategies, and information overload would help in preparing design guidelines for system implementers.

2) Menu selection - menu selection is offered on many systems for novice users, but there is little data to support design guidelines. The content, number, placement, and phrasing of menu choices could be studied with attention to titling of menu frames, effectiveness of instructions, availability of type-ahead strategies or menu shortcuts, backtracking, and graphic design to show hierarchical organization. Much progress could be made in this area with modest experimental efforts. There is also an

opportunity to investigate software architectures for menu
management systems, which dramatically reduce the amount of code
while permitting end users to develop and maintain their own
menus.

3) Command languages - this traditional style of interaction is
another excellent candidate for research to understand the importance of consistency in syntactic format, congruent pairings of
commands, hierarchical structure, choice of familiar command
names and parameters, suitable abbreviated forms, automatic
command completion, and interference from multiple routes to
accomplish the same task. The impact of response time and novel
hardware display and entry devices on the command set is another
worthy topic.

4) Graceful evolution - although novices may begin with menu
selection, they may wish to evolve to faster or more powerful
facilities. Methods for smoothing the transition from novice to
intermittent knowledgeable to frequent expert could be studied.
The differing needs of novice and experts in prompting, error
messages, on-line assistance, display complexity, locus of
control, pacing, and informative feedback need investigation.

5) Anxiety and fear of computer usage - although computers are widely used, they still serve only a fraction of the population. Many
people avoid using computerized devices, such as bank terminals
or word processors, because they are anxious or even fearful of
breaking the computer, making an embarrassing mistake or being
incapable of succeeding. Interviews with non-users of computers
would help determine the sources of this anxiety and lead to
design guidelines to alleviate the fear. Tests could be run to
determine the effectiveness of re-design of systems and of
improved training procedures.

6) Specification and implementation of interaction - most interactive systems are constructed with traditional procedural
languages, but novel techniques could reduce implementation times
by an order of magnitude. Specification languages and dialog
management systems have been proposed and some commercial packages are available. Advanced research on tools to aid

interactive systems designers and implementers might have
substantial payoff in reducing costs and improving quality.

7) Direct manipulation - graphical interfaces in which the user
   operates on a representation of the objects of interest are
   extremely attractive in computer assisted design and manufactur-
   ing, video games, database query, electronic spreadsheets,
   display editors, etc. Empirical studies would refine our understanding of what is an appropriate analogical representation and
   the role of rapid, incremental, reversible operations.

8) On-line assistance - although many systems offer some help or
   tutorial information on-line, there is limited understanding of
   what constitutes effective design for novices, intermittent knowledgeable users, and experts. The role of these aids and on-line
   user consultants could be studied to assess their impact on user
   success and satisfaction. The utility of a separate display or
   window for assistance or tutorials should be contrasted with the
   common approach of entering a separate subsystem which displaces
   the current display of work.

9) Hardware devices - the plethora of keyboards, displays, and
   pointing devices presents opportunities and challenges to system
   designers. The heated discussions about the relative merits of
   lightpens, touchscreens, voice input, function keys, or high
   resolution displays could be resolved through extensive experimentation with multiple tasks and user communities. Underlying
   issues include speed, accuracy, fatigue, error correction, and
   subjective satisfaction.

10) Programming style - comprehensibility of programs is effected by
    cosmetic issues such as commenting, indentation, choice of
    mnemonic names, and use of blank space. Structural issues such as
    number of arguments in a module, global vs. local variables,
    nested conditionals vs. expanded Boolean expressions, use of
    pointers, structured control structures, and data abstraction
    also influence comprehensibility. Although studies have been
    performed for some of these issues much work remains.

11) Programmer workstations - programmer productivity might be
    substantially raised by an improved workstation. Rapid response

time, high resolution graphics, high-speed printers, adequate on-line library facilities, advanced editors, program analysis tools, and advanced debugging software need to be implemented, tested, and refined for the professional programmer environment.

12) Program documentation - many organizations have standards for internal and external documentation, but realistic evaluations of effectiveness are rare. Comprehensive trials of documentation style for control flow, data structures, module interfaces, concurrency, and real time constraints would produce guidelines to practitioners and insights to the cognitive processes of program comprehension. A major beneficiary of these results would be program maintenance organizations.

9. GOALS

Clear goals are useful, not only for system development, but also for educational and professional enterprises. In the past decade, I have been working on human factors issues with three primary goals - influencing academic and industrial researchers, providing tools, techniques and knowledge for commercial systems implementers, and raising the consciousness of the general public.

Influencing academic and industrial researchers

Early research in human-computer interaction was done largely by introspection and intuition, but this approach suffered from lack of validity, generality, and precision. By applying the techniques of controlled psychologically oriented experimentation, I believe we can obtain a deeper understanding of the fundamental principles of human interaction with computers.

The reductionist scientific method has this basic outline:

- lucid statement of a testable hypothesis
- manipulation of a small number of independent variables
- measurement of specific dependent variables
- careful selection and assignment of subjects
- control for biasing
- application of statistical tests

Materials and methods must be tested by pilot experiments and results must be validated by replication in variant situations.

Of course, the highly developed and structured method of controlled experimentation has its weaknesses. It may be difficult or expensive to find adequate subjects and laboratory-like conditions may distort the situation so much that the conclusions have no application. When results for large groups of subjects are arrived at by statistical aggregation, extremely good or poor performance by individuals may be overlooked. Furthermore, anecdotal evidence or individual insights may be given too little emphasis, because of the authoritative impact of statistics.

In spite of these concerns, controlled experimentation provides a productive basis which can be modified to suit the situation. Anecdotal experiences and subjective reactions should be recorded, thinking aloud or protocol approaches should be employed, field or case studies with extensive performance data collection should be carried out, and the individual insights of researchers, designers, and experimental participants should be captured.

Within computer science, there is a growing awareness of the need for greater attention to human factors issues. Researchers who propose new programming language or data structure constructs are more aware of the need to match human cognitive skills. Developers of advanced graphics systems, robots, computer assisted design systems, or artificial intelligence applications increasingly recognize that the success of their proposals depends on the construction of a suitable human interface. Researchers in these and other areas are making efforts to understand and measure human performance.

In psychology, there is a grand opportunity to apply the knowledge and techniques of traditional psychology, and recent subfields such as cognitive psychology, to the study of human-computer interaction. Psychologists are investigating human problem solving with computers to gain an understanding of cognitive processes and memory structures. The benefit to psychology is great, but psychologists also have the golden opportunity to dramatically influence an important and widely used technology.

Researchers in information science, business and management, education, sociology and in other disciplines are benefitting and contrib-
uting by their study of human-computer interaction.

Tools and techniques for systems developers

Commercial systems managers, designers, and implementers are emerging
from benign neglect of human engineering. There is a great thirst for
knowledge, for software tools, for design guidelines, and for testing
techniques. Dialog management software packages are appearing to
provide support for rapid prototype and system development, while
aiding design consistency and simplifying evolutionary refinement or
maintenance. Guidelines documents are being written for general audi-
ences and for specific applications. Many projects are taking the
productive route of writing their own guidelines specifically tied to
the problems of their application environment. These guidelines are
constructed from experimental results, experience with actual
systems, and some knowledgeable guesswork.

Pilot and acceptance testing is appropriate during system
development. Once the initial system is available refinements can be
made on the basis of on-line or printed surveys, individual or group
interviews, or from more controlled empirical tests of novel strategies.

Feedback from users during the development process and for evolutionary refinement can provide useful insights and guidance. An on-line
electronic mail facility allows users to send comments directly to
the designers. On-line user consultants can provide prompt assistance
and much information about the activity and problems of the user
community.

Raising the consciousness of the general public

The media is so filled with stories about computers, that public
consciousness raising may seem unnecessary. But in fact, many people
are anxious and fearful about using computers. When they do finally
use a bank terminal or word processor they are fearful of making
mistakes, anxious about breaking the computer, worried about feeling
incompetent, or threatened by the computer "being smarter than I am".
These fears are justified, in part, by the poor designs which have

complex syntactic forms, hostile, condemning, and unhelpful messages, and the misleading anthropomorphic style of some systems.

Part of my effort has been devoted to educating the general public to put their internal fears into action. Instead of feeling guilty or inadequate when they get a message like "SYNTAX ERROR", they should express their anger at the system designer who was so inconsiderate and thoughtless. As examples of successful and satisfying systems become more visible, the crude designs will appear increasingly archaic and become commercial failures. As designers improve interactive systems, some of these fears will recede and the positive experience of competence, mastery, and satisfaction will flow in. Then the image of computer scientists and data processing professionals will change in the public's view. The machine oriented and technical image will give way to one of personal warmth, sensitivity and concern for the user.

10. PRACTITIONER'S SUMMARY

If you are working on a project where there is substantial concern for short learning times, rapid task performance, low error rates, user satisfaction, and ease of retention, then you should set measurable goals with pilot studies and acceptance tests. There is a rapidly growing literature and sets of design guidelines which may be of assistance. Each new application has its special cases and you can keep on course by involving users during the design, through development, and for evolutionary refinement. Error frequency data and command utilization statistics are useful in tuning the system. Subjective satisfaction can be measured through on-line or printed surveys, while unstructured feedback can be obtained from electronic mail and user consultants.

11. RESEARCHER'S AGENDA

The opportunities for researchers are unlimited. There are so many interesting, important, and doable projects, that it may be hard to choose a direction. Begin by understanding the practical background of the problem, consider the fundamental psychological principles of human behavior, and propose a lucid, testable hypothesis. Then consider the appropriate research methodology, collect the data, and analyze the results. Finally, return to the practical application area with specific recommendations and refine your model of human performance.

GUIDELINES DOCUMENTS

Engel, Stephen E. and Granda, Richard E., Guidelines for Man/Display Interfaces, Technical Report TR 00.2720, IBM, Poughkeepsie, N.Y. (December 1975).

--An early and influential document which is the basis for several of the other guidelines documents.

Smith, Sid L., User-System Interface Design for Computer-Based Information Systems, Report ESD-TR-82-132. The MITRE Corporation, Bedford, MA 01730, Electronic Systems Division, (April 1982), 181 pages.

--This thorough document, which is continuously being revised, begins with a good discussion of human factors issues in design and then covers data entry, data display, and sequence control. Guidelines are offered with comments, examples, exceptions, and references. Sid Smith is seeking comments for refinement and expansion, telephone 617-271-7768.

Human Engineering Design Criteria for Military Systems, Equipment and Facilities, Military Standard MIL-STD-1472C, U.S. Government Printing Office, (May 2, 1981).

--Almost three hundred pages, largely on traditional ergonometric or anthropometric issues, but this latest edition has a ten page addition on "Personnel-Computer interface".

Human Factors Review of Electric Power Dispatch Control Centers: Volume 2 Detailed Survey Results, Prepared by Lockheed Missiles and Space Company for the Electric Power Research Institute, 3412 Hillview Avenue, Palo Alto, CA 94304, 1981.

--Well researched and thoughtful comments about electric power control centers, with many generally applicable conclusions.

Human Factors of Work Stations with Display Terminals, IBM Document G 320-6102-1, San Jose, CA 95193 (1979).

--Informative and readable discussion about terminal design.

Human Factors Engineering Criteria for Information Processing Systems, Lockheed Missiles and Space Company, Inc., Sunnyvale, CA 94086 (September 1982)

--Well written and precise guidelines with numerous examples on display format, data entry, language and coding, interaction sequence control, error handling procedures, on-line guidance, and color displays. Available from C. Marlin Brown, Orgn. 62-91, Bldg. 538, Telephone 408-742-4399.

BOOKS

Badre, Albert, and Shneiderman, Ben (Editors), "Directions in Human-Computer Interaction", Ablex Publishing Co., Norwood, NJ, (1980).

Bailey, Robert W., Human Performance Engineering: A Guide for System Designers, Prentice-Hall, Incl., Englewood Cliffs, NJ, (1982).

Cakir, A., Hart, D.J., and Stewart, T.F.M., Visual Display Terminals: A Manual Covering Ergonomics, Workplace Design, Health and Safety, Task Organization, John Wiley and Sons, New York, NY, (1980).

Foley, James D., and Van Dam, Andries, Fundamentals of Interactive Computer Graphics, Addison-Wesley Publishing Co., Reading, MA, (1982).

Guedj, R. (Editor), Methodology of Interaction, North-Holland Publishing Co., Amsterdam, (1980).

Hiltz, Starr Roxanne, and Turroff, Murray, The Network Nation: Human Communication via Computer, Addison-Wesley Publishing Co., Reading, MA, (1978).

Larson, James A. (Editor), Tutorial: End User Facilities in the 1980's, IEEE Computer Society Press (EHO 198-2), New York, NY, (1982).

Martin, James, Design of Man-computer Dialogues, Prentice-Hall, Inc., Englewood Cliffs, NJ, (1973).

Mehlmann, Marilyn, When People Use Computers: An Approach to Developing an Interface, Prentice-Hall, Incl., Englewood Cliffs, NJ, (1981).

Shneiderman, Ben, Software Psychology: Human Factors in Computer and Information Systems, Little Brown and Co., Boston, MA, (1980).

Smith, H.T., and Green, T.R.G. (Editors), Human Interaction with Computers, Academic Press, New York, NY, (1980).

Welford, A.T., Skilled Performance: Perceptual and Motor skills, Scott, Foresman and Co., Glenview, IL, (1976).

ARTICLES

Allen, R., Cognitive factors in human interaction with computers, In Badre, A., and Shneiderman, B. (Editors), Directions in Human-Computer Interaction. Ablex Publishing Co., Norwood, NJ, (1982).

Card, Stuart, English, William, and Burr, Betty, Evaluation of mouse, rate-controlled isometric joystick, step keys, and text keys for text selection on a CRT. Ergonomics 21(8), (1978), 601-613.

Card, S.K., Moran, T.P., and Newell, A., The keystroke-level model for user performance with interactive systems, Communications of the ACM 23, (1980), 396-410.

Chapanis, Alphonse, Words, words, words. Human Factors 7(1), (1965), 1-17.

Clark, I.A., Software simulation as a tool for usable product design, IBM Systems Journal 20(3), (1981), 272-293.

Doherty, W.J., and Kelisky, R.P., Managing VM/CMS systems for user effectiveness, IBM Systems Journal 18(1), (1979), 143-163.

Durding, B.M., Becker, C.A., and Gould, J.D., Data organization, Human Factors 19, (1977), 1-14.

Durrett, John, and Trezona, Judi, How to use color displays effectively, BYTE, (April 1982), 50-53.

Embley, David W., and Nagy, George, Behavioral aspects of text editors, ACM Computing Surveys 13(1), (March 1981), 33-70.

Ledgard, Henry, Whiteside, John, Singer, Andrew, and Seymour, William, The natural language of interactive systems, Communications of the ACM, 23(10), (October 1980), 556-563.

Miller, Lance, and Thomas Jr., J.C., Behavioral issues in the use of interactive systems, International Journal of Man-Machine Studies 9, (1977), 509-536.

Reisner, Phyllis, Human factors studies of database query languages: A survey and assessment, ACM Computing Surveys 13(1), (March 1981), 13-31.

Robertson, P.J., A guide to using color on alphanumeric displays, IBM Technical Report G320-6296-0, IBM White Plains, NY, (1980).

Rouse, William B., Human-computer interaction in the control of dynamic systems, ACM Computing Surveys 13(1), (March 1981), 71-100.

Shneiderman, Ben, The future of interactive systems and the emergence of direct manipulation, Behaviour and Information Technology, (to appear) and Vassiliou, Y. (Editor), Human Factors of Interactive Computer Systems, Ablex Publishing Co., Norwood, NJ, (1983).

Shneiderman, Ben, Designing computer system messages, Communications of the ACM, 25(9), (September 1982), 610-611.

Shneiderman, Ben, Multiparty grammars and related features for defining interactive systems, IEEE Transactions on System, Man, and Cybernetics SMC 12(2), (March/April 1982), 148-154.

Shneiderman, Ben, Human factors experiments in designing interactive systems, IEEE Computer, 12(12), (1979), 9-19.

Thadhani, A.J., Interactive user productivity, IBM Systems Journal 20(4), (1981), 407-423.

Thomas, John C., and Carrol, J.M., Human factors in communication, IBM Systems Journal 20, (1981), 237-263.

THE INTEGRATED DATA ANALYSIS AND

MANAGEMENT SYSTEM -

A GENERATOR FOR ENDUSER SYSTEMS

U. Schauer
IBM Scientific Center
Tiergartenstr. 15
D-6900 Heidelberg

ABSTRACT: The Integrated Data Analysis and Management System (IDAMS)
was developed at the Heidelberg Scientific Center to support enduser
application specialists in interactive non-routine usage and manipulation of large data collections. It evolved into an Enduser System
Generator which allows to conceive, design and build applications
exploiting the system's facilities for interactive data manipulation
and for creation of application specific procedures.

The following discussions put special emphasis on the design issues
and the principles which were applied to provide a coherent interface
to both programmers and non-programmers, extensible to specific
application needs, and adaptive to the user's knowledge and developing programming skill. Following a short introduction the discussion
will focus on IDAMS' high level query language, on issues of interactive user guidance, on the process of extension and customization,
with some conclusions based on observations in actual usage.

The process of application development by DP professionals, i. e.
design, creation, and maintenance of data bases and application packages is not elaborated.The emphasis is put on the system's facilities
allowing an enduser to create his own simple applications.

1. Introduction

Large quantities of measurement data have been accumulated or are
still under development in science and industry. These data may apply
to virtually every application, whether purely scientific like experiments in physics, medicine etc. or business oriented as, e. g.,
forecasting, resource planning, and accounting. The detailed analysis and non-routine usage of such data collections by technical or
business professional end users (scientists, engineers, economists -
with little or no programming skill and ambitions) has heavy demands
for

o   a powerful interactive language
o   a flexible data base management system
o   comfortable and versatile report formatting
o   easy embedding of application specific algorithms
o   rich facilities for graphical display of data
o   on-line usage-information on system, programs and data
o   application oriented description of data and programs.

The Integrated Data Analysis and Management System (IDAMS) has coherent offerings for all the above requirements. It is heavily based on
APL and derives many of its virtues directly from APL's excellence
for interactive problem solving. Without APL's rich array handling
facilities application programs could not be embedded easily.

IDAMS   provides   major   enhancements   to   APL's   problem   solving
facilities: Access to a data base system, XRM [LOR74] or System R
[CHA76]; efficient execution of non-APL programs by an auxiliary
processor [EBE77]; a coherent interface to Data Analysis and Management suitable for non-programmers; a systematized documentation
discipline for data and programs.

Unique features [RDS 83] of IDAMS' non-procedural query language are
the support of a tabular data model, with array structures on the
field level, the symmetrical treatment of tables and functions, and
an option for automatic handling of units attached to data.

IDAMS may be viewed as a generator for enduser systems since it
provides an interactive working environment supporting the intelligence, design and choice phases of interactive problem solving
[CAS 74], [MUE 83]. This means that it supports users in performing
the following tasks:

o Create a better understanding of the problem under investigation.
  Major tasks are identification of pertinent data and programs,
  followed by collection, manipulation and display of data.

o Explore "what if"-type questions. Investigation of the problem's
  dependencies is the major theme. Programs needed for solution
  become developed and important problem parameters get identified.

o Establish a commonly agreed solution process, implemented as an application program, and built upon data and programs of the previous steps.

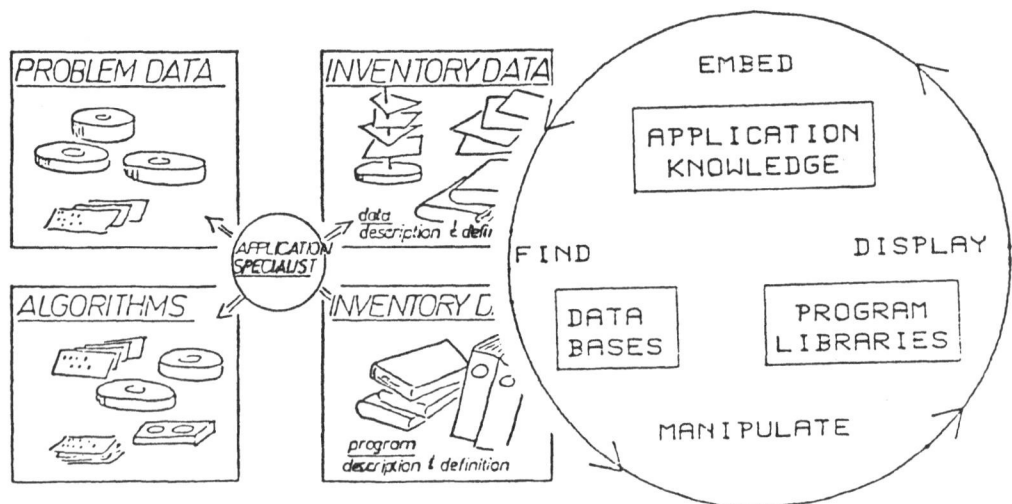

Figure 1 illustrates needs and major activities of interactive problem solving.

Giving equal emphasis to data and programs introduces a systematization to problem solving in which application knowledge plays a central role. It covers information on programs and data, but also offers an opportunity to integrate application programs into a self explanatory, coherent offering by introducing additional information layers. The expertise of application developing users is made available to others using the embedded application programs.

2. Query Language Design Considerations

In modeling the non-procedural query language of IDAMS, which expresses the data flow between tables, functions, and input or output devices, several predicate types must be distinguished. For a uniform presentation and visualization of these predicates, skeletons, as used in Query by Example [ZLO 74] are conceivably most appropriate. Data flow may involve calculation, therefore some notions of basic algebra are also needed. Adding the concepts of constant values, variables, and of calculational expressions (in terms of constants and variables) the essential features of the language are specified. Allowing for expressions formulated through APL the language is well defined and also allows for extension and adaptation by those familiar with APL. An additional skeleton type, which covers the predicates expressing constraints, completes the two dimensional display oriented query language with a minimum of concepts and special rules.

2.1 Functional Facilities of Query

In the following "query" is used in the wider sense of interactive problem solving. Major tasks attributed to query are:

o Extract, manipulate, and perform calculations on tabular data
o Create tabular results and new tables
o Build functions as needed for developing application programs
o Update and maintain tables

Actually the above tasks will be performed by a combination of the following steps:

SELECT object   - identify and select tables and functions
DEFINE query   - specify data extraction, manipulation, and presen-
                   tation
COMPILE query   - generate an executable function, checking for
                   correctness
RUN query   - monitored execution with prompts for inputs and
                   error recovery
SHOW result   - allow for various presentations of a tabular result
MODIFY query   - reenter query definition with an already existing
                   query
SAVE query   - allow for repeated usage or for modification of a
                   query

Except for the COMPILE step any of the above operations may be extended to other objects. RUN and SHOW remain restricted to func- tions and tables respectively, but the others apply to any object.

The SAVE command would be incomplete without a COPY facility. Together-
er SAVE and COPY allow to distinguish between a temporary and a
permanent version of an object. This concept provides a backout
facility for temporary data changes, which may be necessary to investigate "what if"-type questions. SAVE and COPY obviously apply to
query, result, function and table.

2.2 Useability Considerations for Query

A set of commands as sketched above is the hard core of the facilities of IDAMS. Availability of a display screen allows to model the
command syntax in terms of panel operations. The user actions are
then as simple as to select from a menu and to enter responses in
compliance with system prompts. Consistent design of such panels is
of major concern.

Full screen editor facilities are mandatory for the definition mode
entered by the DEFINE command. Quick response is also essential.
Required editor facilities are scrolling and insert, delete, and copy
of lines. Anything disruptive to the editing process must be avoided,
e. g. entering long fields should not present a major problem.

The definition process must be interruptible, allowing to exploit
user guidance, or to use APL for some auxiliary calculations, or for
verifying proper understanding of some APL expression. Interruptibil-
ity is also desirable during panel driven operations. On-line guidance must provide information at least on visible objects and
applicable commands.

Consistency with APL-terminology is important since the query
language encompasses APL, and compiled queries are truly APL functions. Extensibility of the query language and adaptation to developing APL knowledge are then obtained without additional effort.

Nearly as important as consistency are simplicity and comprehensiveness. Only few panel types should be used and menu offerings must
always be given with proper sorting and intelligible grouping.
Predictability must apply to sequences of panels performing a task,
to the handling of exceptional conditions, and to defaulting.

2.3 Concepts and Rules of Query

Objects of IDAMS' non-procedural high level query language are:

constants - e. g. number, numeric vector, character string
variables - denoted by names starting with a character
tables   - name followed by column identifiers
functions - name followed by input/output parameters

The query language exploits APL for formulation of predicates and thus encompasses the full power of its host language APL. The rules of APL apply for forming constants and variables. A compiler transforms queries from their non-procedural definition form into executable APL functions; this avoids introduction of new objects and allows to build nested queries.

The following skeleton types are used:

o Condition - for specification of constraints
o Table   - for controlling selection of and access to data
o Result   - for accumulation of resultant data
o Function   - to calculate outputs for given inputs
o Query   - to specify name and input/output parameters

From a syntactic point of view three different skeleton types are sufficient:

```
    Table/Result:          NAME | COLUMNNAMES | ...
                                |               |

    Function/Query:        NAME | INPUTS | ... || OUTPUTS | ...
                                |        |     ||          |

    Condition:             APL | EXPRESSIONS
                               |
```

But, semantically one has to distinguish carefully between table and result skeletons and between function and query skeletons. The query skeleton will always be used on top of the screen as kind of a function header line. The default offering for the query skeleton is QUERY. Result skeletons, if any, are also part of the query

interface.   Therefore they will be put   next to the   query skeleton.
This order helps to disambiguate between query and other function
skeletons and between result and table skeletons.

The following rules apply:

(1) A query may use zero, one,   or several of table skeletons, result
    skeletons, and function skeletons.
(2) There is exactly one query skeleton describing the query name and
    its interface, i.e. input and output parameters of the query, if
    any.
(3) Query and result skeletons may become changed, no guidance
    applies yet. Other skeletons must not be changed, on-line guid-
    ance is available.
(4) Predicates formulated through APL, generally constraints and
    definitions, are listed in the condition skeleton.

Binding rules apply to variables:

(1) All variables must be bound, e. g.   to the domain of values of a
    table column, or to a constant value.
(2) A variable appearing in an input column of the query skeleton or
    in a table column is bound. A variable may also become bound by
    an equality predicate, if the equation's other side is bound.
(3) Rows in a result skeleton must have one entry for each column.
    They do not imply any binding.
(4) A function reference must have all its inputs bound. Outputs are
    bound if all inputs got proper binding.
(5) A query skeleton with parameters must have a row entered with
    bound outputs, if any.

Each row in a skeleton expresses a predicate.   Predicates in
non-result skeletons are connected by an implicit "and" condition,
they have to hold true simultaneously. The rows in a result (table)
skeleton express predicates which are combined through an implied
"or" condition.   Result tables comprise sets of tuples and the
implied "or" models the process of set union.

Without loss of generality one might restrict all skeleton entries to
variable names with the exception of the condition skeleton. However,
this most simple rule causes introduction of unwanted variable names,

e. g. for every constant value. Therefore the most permissive rule
is used instead. Variables are then only needed to specify data flow
and computations, or for abbreviation purposes:

Every skeleton entry may be an APL expression (exceptions will be
stated explicitly). For compilation this is mapped to the simpler
case above. The expression gets substituted by a system generated
variable and the predicate <variable> = <expression> is added to the
condition skeleton. The rule remains simple if one further allows
the expression to be prefixed by a comparison operator
(>, $\geq$, <, $\leq$, =, $\neq$). In this case the comparison operator will
replace the equal sign in the generated predicate above. The default
assumption is for an equal sign as prefix.

2.4 Example for Use of Query

Let NAME denote a table containing short abbreviation, long name, and
industry code of companies. The query task is then initialized by
SELECT TABLE NAME which brings up the query definition screen ready
for user insertions.

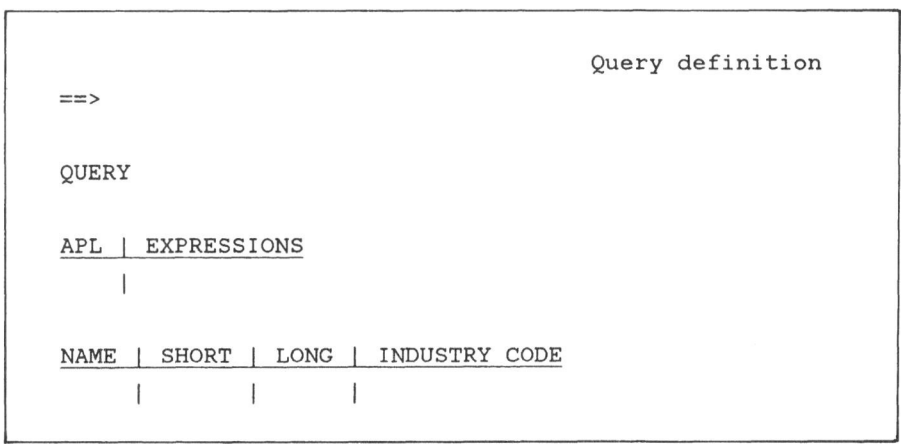

Our user wants a RESULT table with columns INDUSTRY ID NAME ... He
enters RESULT (INDUSTRY,ID,NAME) underneath QUERY and pushes the
enter key. The screen will change to

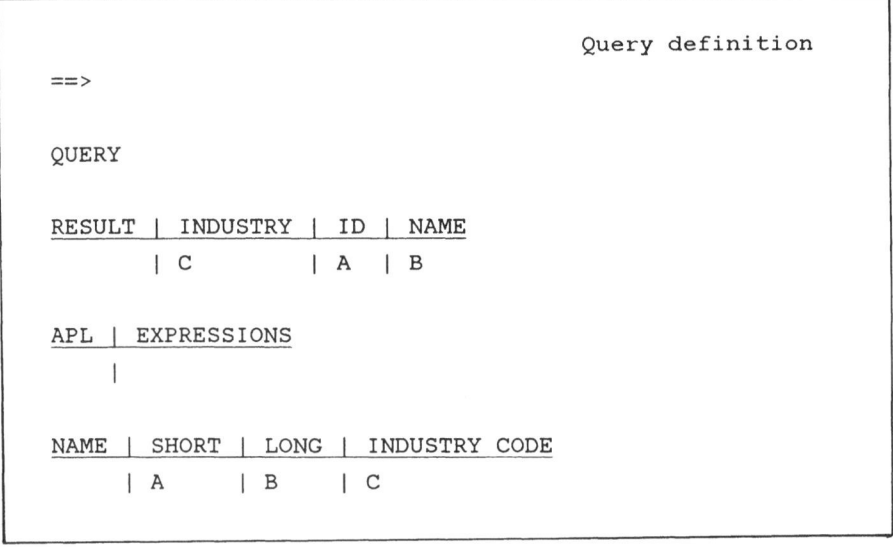

Using three variables, e. g., A, B, C our user now specifies the data flow from NAME to RESULT

Having done so he pushes function key PF3, which always has the meaning "close" the current action. He could also enter the command COMPILE and then press enter. Only the top line of the screen changes into Query compilation.

After successful compilation the second line shows the default for continuation, i. e. ===> RUN QUERY and the third line reads: "successful compilation, press enter to continue." The user still has the option to change the default operation. In case of errors a diagnostic message appears and the process is put back to the Query definition stage.

If the user presses enter the RUN-command gets effective and the top line changes to Query execution. Query execution will result in the display of the RESULT table. Query execution may take considerable time, therefore some TRACE option is desirable. It could be attached to the RESULT table, to the RUN command or to the user's profile, meaning that display takes place, when the RESULT table has grown by a specified amount. With each intermediate display the user has the option to cancel or continue the execution.

```
                                            Query execution
    ==>


    RESULT


    INDUSTRY   ID   NAME
    BAN             CBK COMMERZBANK
    PRO             SCH SCHERING
    PRO             BAS BASF (BADISCHE ANILIN UND SODAFABRIK)
    AUT             KHD KLOECKNER HUMBOLDT DEUTZ
    AUT             NSU AUDI NSU
    PRO             BAY BAYER LEVERKUSEN
    ELE             SEL STANDARD ELEKTRIK LORENZ
    BAN             ALL ALLIANZ VERSICHERUNG
    ELE             AEG ALLGEMEINE ELEKTRIZITAETSGESELLSCHAFT
    AUT             DAI DAIMLER-BENZ
    PRO             CAS CASSELLA FARBWERKE MAINKUR
    PRO             HFA HOECHST AG
    BAN             DBK DEUTSCHE BANK
    BAN             DRB DRESDNER BANK
    AUT             BMW BAYRISCHE MOTORENWERKE
```

The role of the top three lines is self explanatory. The top line informs about the current status. The third line is for informative messages and diagnostics. The second line allows to enter commands. The very same control part can be associated to every panel used for communication. The user then always has the control option to enter one of the supported commands. The control part allows to visualize the next operation using the same interface style in a consistent way. Change of the default continuation is made easy and comprehensible.

An overview of all possible commands can be obtained by setting the cursor into the command entry field (this is achieved by pushing PF12) and then pushing PF1 for help. If the cursor is in the NAME column of a skeleton then PF1 causes display of the whole object's description, while cursor positioning in another column will restrict the description to the pertinent column. The description overwrites part of the screen. PF3 may be used to "close" this display action.

Possible commands would be those driving the editor facilities but also the SELECT, SAVE, RUN, DEFINE, MODIFY, SHOW, COPY commands introduced above. APL commands are acceptable if starting with a special symbol, e. g. the execute symbol. Alternatively a PF-key could be used to signal an interrupt to the APL facility.

Our RESULT-table contains all tuples of the NAME-table but in non-specified order. The sequence of columns and the column headings were specified explicitly. The query became compiled into an APL function with the name QUERY as requested by the default query skeleton QUERY (without input/output parameters).

Our user finds it difficult to use the RESULT-table, since he wanted to look at process industry only. With the MODIFY command he reenters query definition and adds C ='PRO' in the condition skeleton. As result of the RUN step he will now obtain a RESULT table containing only the names belonging to the process industry.

For ease of use commands may have default parameter specifications, depending on the context. MODIFY as applied above without parameters means, when applied in the query execution stage to reenter the query definition mode for the "current" query. The interpretation of current preferably is "the query under execution" and not "the last compiled query".

The concept of a parametric query is exploited next. The parametric query to be developed shall allow to display any industry without the overhead of query definition and compilation.

Using the MODIFY option again our user deletes the condition line and overwrites QUERY by LIST CODE, where LIST is his proposed query name and CODE associates a right hand input parameter to the LIST function. Pushing "enter" the query skeleton appears, ready for entering C.

LIST | CODE
     | C

At the RUN step the user will now get a prompt message to enter his desired value for CODE. He enters 'PRO' and gets

```
                                            Query execution
   ==>
   enter values for input parameters of LIST
   CODE <- 'PRO'


   RESULT


   INDUSTRY   ID  NAME
   PRO           SCH SCHERING
   PRO           BAS BASF (BADISCHE ANILIN UND SODAFABRIK)
   PRO           BAY BAYER LEVERKUSEN
   PRO           CAS CASSELLA FARBWERKE MAINKUR
   PRO           HFA HOECHST AG
```

The parametric query LIST could also be used from APL in the form LIST 'PRO' to produce a display of the result table. There is no difference between the prompt input and the right hand parameter value of LIST above. The same rules apply. The response to the prompt for input to CODE may be any APL expression, which evaluates to an industry code as used in the NAME-table. The interface of compiled queries strictly adheres to the rules of APL. LIST is an APL function with a right hand parameter, which produces a tabular display.

For a full modelling of the APL-interface of queries the following syntax is used:

<APL call form> (<global parameters>)

<APL call form> specifies name and explicit parameters:

<result> <- <left parameter> <u>query name></u> <right parameter>

<global parameters> specifies the global parameters:

<input parameter list> -> <output parameter list>.

2.5 Additional Features of Query

Result skeletons are used to define tabular results. A resultant table is therefore ready for being saved in the database. Special presentation requests for sorting, grouping, or counting and subtotaling cannot be expressed with the non-procedural language developed so far. However, they can become specified easily by adding presentation requests to the RESULT skeleton.

2.5.1 Refined Reporting

The following presentation attributes are offered

ORDER   -   for special sorting of rows
              A for ascending, D for descending.
GROUP   -   for hierarchical grouping
              1 for highest level, 2 for second level, etc.
TOTAL   -   to handle calculation requests on groups
              C for count, S for sum, L for low, H for high, A for average.
APPEAR   -   to enable duplicate control
              O for omit, K for keep.
ASSIGN   -   to return result columns in variables
FORMAT   -   to format output specifically

The keywords are entered in the front column and the affected columns get properly marked. An ASSIGN request means that those columns which have a variable name entered will become aggregated into an array and assigned to the variable. Assigned variables may be used as result variables of the query. ORDER will be reflected in assigned variables but not GROUP. FORMAT allows the specification of format elements for data items. The format elements are defined in consistency with APL. The role of the APPEAR attribute is to provide a

means for explicit control of duplicate rows in the tabular display
and also in the assigned variables.

The ASSIGN facility will structure scalar entries into a column
vector, i.e. a matrix with one column, and vector entries also into a
matrix. This seemingly inconsistent shape-rule was chosen to retain
the presentation shape on the display. The user gets objects as he
perceives them on the screen.

Specification of ORDER and GROUP could be included as shown below

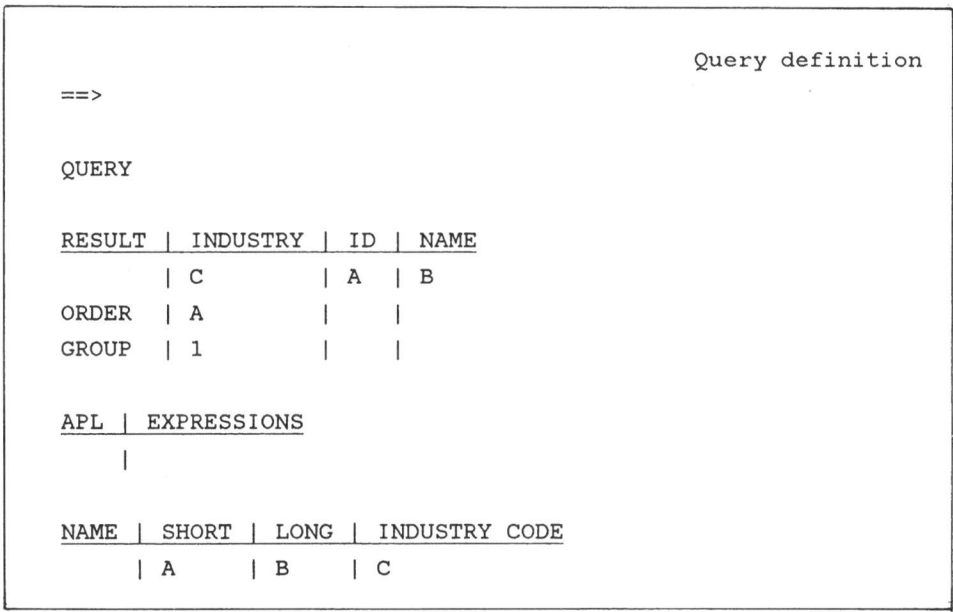

Query execution will then present the RESULT-table grouped by the
first column, which is also used as major key for sorting to ascending ORDER.
The RESULT table remains a relation, unaffected by ORDER and GROUP
requests. However, columns assigned to variables would become arrays
reflecting the order.

```
                                                        Query execution

   ==>


   RESULT


   INDUSTRY  ID  NAME
   AUT          BMW BAYRISCHE MOTORENWERKE
                KHD KLOECKNER HUMBOLDT DEUTZ
                DAI DAIMLER BENZ
                NSU AUDI NSU
   BAN          CBK COMMERZBANK
                DBK DEUTSCHE BANK
                DRB DRESDNER BANK
                ALL ALLIANZ VERSICHERUNG
   ELE          SEL STANDARD ELEKTRIK LORENZ
                AEG ALLGEMEINE ELEKTRIZITAETSGESELLSCHAFT
   PRO          BAS BASF(BADISCHE ANILIN- UND SODAFABRIK
                BAY BAYER LEVERKUSEN
                CAS CASSELLA FARBWERKE MAINKUR
                HFA HOECHST AG
                SCH SCHERING
```

The overhead of query compilation and execution is not needed to achieve different presentations of a result table.

A change of the presentation of the RESULT table to alphabetic sorting within the groups can be requested by the SHOW RESULT command and successive specifications. The SHOW command always needs the table name as parameter. It brings up the table skeleton, with the presentation offerings, ready for specification of presentation requests.

RESULT	INDUSTRY	ID	NAME
ORDER	A	A	
GROUP	1		
TOTAL			
APPEAR			
ASSIGN			
FORMAT			

The above specification is self explanatory and needs minimal
keystrokes. The ID column is now used additionally as minor sorting
key.

Refined reporting can be requested at query definition time or as an
afterthought having seen the standard presentation of the result
table. Command defaulting does not apply for SHOW since a query may
have several result tables and then any default rule would be very
questionable.

2.5.2 Use of Aggregation

The grouping operation could also be achieved using aggregation.
APL's array handling facilities offer an easy possibility to apply
functions on the aggregated groups, e. g., average, standard devi-
ation, top 3. This gives much more flexibility and functional power
than the refined reporting facility. However, for simple requests the
refined reporting offer is easier to use. It can also become implemented more efficiently. Aggregation together with APL's array
handling provides the functional power of the hyperrelational model
of data proposed in [CHN75].

Aggregation is one of the most important tabular operations, meaning
to select all rows of a table having fixed entries in one or several
specified columns and to retain the imposed aggregation of the values
in one or several other specified columns. The entries in an aggregation predicate must be marked fixed or aggregated. This can be
accomplished by prefixing the names of the variables to be aggregated
by a non-alphabetic character. The choice of this prefix character
is not arbitrary. It must not introduce ambiguities.

The nil-sign of APL is a possible choice. It was preferred to the
also possible period-character for reasons of better visibility.

Period would be the choice on a terminal without APL keyboard. A special panel offering allows to choose between such alternatives, i.e. to set up and adapt the working environment.

Without loss of generality one may restrict entries in an aggregation predicate to variable names for both classes, fixed and aggregated. To be consistently permissive for skeleton entries the unmarked entries (fixed) may also be expressions.

Aggregation predicates are restricted to tables. They introduce an additional binding rule. For convenience reasons the unmarked variables, if any, become bound. This decision is made to minimize the user's surprise. The aggregation predicate could also be handled by the rules for a function predicate (implying that unmarked variables must be bound).

Still better visibility of aggregation could be accomplished by marking aggregation predicates with some keyword e. g. ALL in the first skeleton column. The price to be paid would be additionally required key strokes. This was considered intolerable for the expectedly frequent usage of the aggregation facility.

The following parametric query illustrates the use of aggregation and APL subscripting.

```
┌──────────────────────────────────────────────────────────────────┐
│                                                   Query definition │
│   ==>                                                              │
│                                                                    │
│                                                                    │
│   MONTHLY │ MONTH │ YEAR │ COMPANY ││  RAW  │ ADJUSTED             │
│           │ M     │ Y    │ C       ││ R[,I] │ A[,I]                │
│                                                                    │
│                                                                    │
│   APL │ EXPRESSIONS                                                │
│       │                                                            │
│                                                                    │
│                                                                    │
│   STOCK │ SHORT NAME │ RAW RATES │ ADJUSTED RATES                  │
│         │ C          │ R         │ A                               │
│                                                                    │
│   DATE │ INDEX │ DAY │ MONTH │ YEAR                                │
│        │ oI    │     │ M     │ Y                                   │
│                                                                    │
└──────────────────────────────────────────────────────────────────┘
```

STOCK denotes a table containing time series data of stock quotations, e. g., spanning the period from 1962 to 1982, and DATE is a table which allows to associate the time series index to calendar information. On a terminal without APL feature a function for subsetting with the call interface R <- I SUBSETOF X
would allow to replace R[,I] and A[,I] by I SUBSETOF R and I SUBSETOF A respectively. Even closer modeling of natural language could be obtained with two functions SUBSET and OF, allowing for SUBSET I OF X.

The predicate in the DATE skeleton requests aggregation of all indexes I for a fixed month M and a fixed year Y.

The parametric query MONTHLY returns the subset of the time series R and A for company C over the period month M in year Y.

The compiled query MONTHLY can be used at the APL interface level as shown below:

```
        COMPANY <- 'DAI'
        MONTH   <- 2
        YEAR    <- 1974
        MONTHLY

        RAW
377  376  370  373  382  382  384  384  382  381
381  368  369  365  366  365  365  367  361  360

        ADJUSTED
282  281  277  279  286  286  287  287  286  285
286  276  277  274  274  274  274  275  270  269
```

Execution following the compile step would automatically prompt for the inputs COMPANY, MONTH, YEAR. Assume MONTHLY has been SAVED. Then with the RUN command the System monitors execution. It provides error checking, presentation of the results, and explanation of the function and of its parameters on option (by cursor setting in combination with PF1).

```
                                                  RUN MONTHLY

    ==>


        Short description of monthly if any


          INPUT PARAMETERS


          COMPANY <- 'DAI'
          MONTH   <-  2
          YEAR    <-  1974


          RESULT PARAMETERS


                RAW
          377  376  370  373  382  382  384  384  382  381
          381  368  369  365  366  365  365  367  361  360


                ADJUSTED
          282  281  277  279  286  286  287  287  286  285
          286  276  277  274  274  274  274  275  270  269
```

2.5.3 Exploitation of Functions

The following query DISPLAY will use the MONTHLY function developed
before and also a PLOT function which models graphical display and a
function SMOOTH for smoothing by a moving average technique. Actually the query also shows the use of a facility for distinguishing
different cases of a calculation process.

```
                                                    Query definition
   ==>


   DISPLAY | MONTH | YEAR | COMPANY | CASE
           | M     | Y    | C       | I


   APL | EXPRESSIONS
    1: | I=1
    2: | I=2


   MONTHLY | MONTH | YEAR | COMPANY || RAW | ADJUSTED
           | C     | Y    | C       || R   | A


   PLOT | TYPE  | GRAPH   | TITLE
    1:  | 3     | R AND A | C, 'RAW AND ADJUSTED'
    2:  | 1     | R AND S | C, 'RAW AND SMOOTHED'


   SMOOTH | TYPE | INPUT || RESULT
       2: | 3    | R     || S
```

This parametric query provides an alternative: If the value of I is 1 then it will display a bar-chart of the RAW and ADJUSTED rates, if I is 2 then it will display a line-plot of the RAW rates together with their local smoothing. The query separates into two independent parts those marked with the label 1 respectively 2 and as common part the function reference in the MONTHLY skeleton. If I is neither 1 nor 2 then the query will have no visible effect. Labels need not be numeric, any identifier string is acceptable. This allows to use the distinguishing values directly as labels.

```
    MONTH    <- 2
    YEAR     <- 1974
    COMPANY  <- 'DAI'
    CASE     <- 1
    DISPLAY
```

generates the first plot below, and
```
    CASE     <- 2
    DISPLAY
```
adds the second plot.

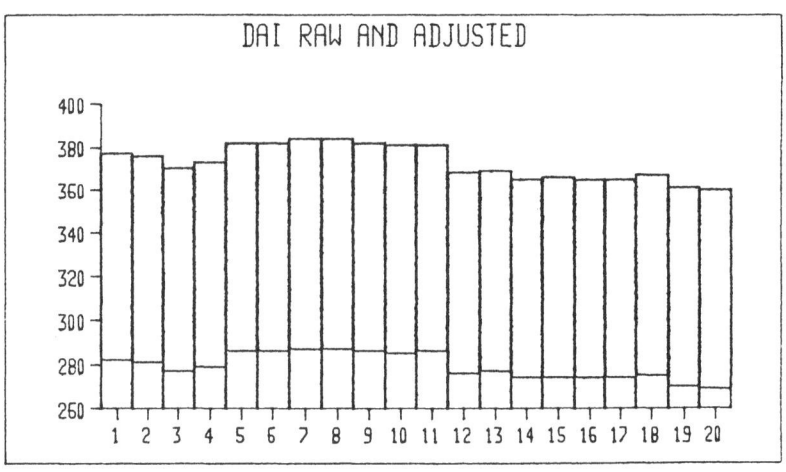

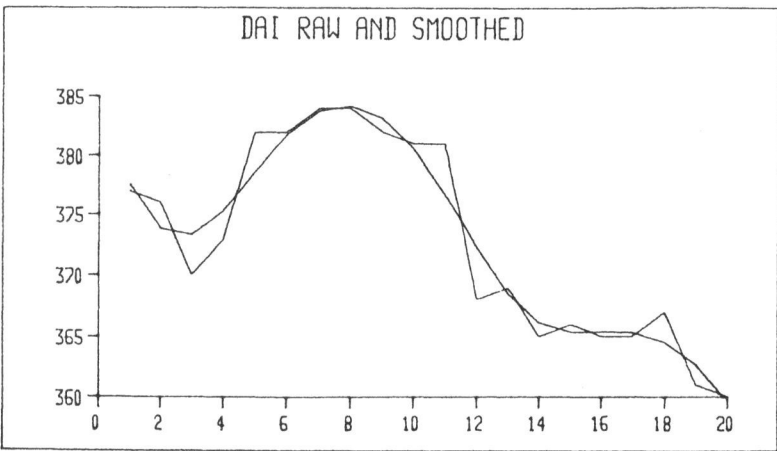

Figure 2. Graphical display facilities

PLOT is a function which controls the graphical output. The TYPE
parameter controls the chart type, e. g.

1 for Line-plot
2 for Scatter-line-plot
3 for Bar-chart

Further presentation attributes may become controlled by specifying
an additional number under TYPE. This number would address an attribute set, which may already exist, or which could be defined during
query definition as one of the next steps, or at the latest possible
time, at query execution. Factoring of attributes allows for custom-

ization of the PLOT interface, especially since the user may introduce meaningful names of his own choice.

Plots are temporarily stored as data structures in their own right. This allows to change presentation attributes, to zoom, and to apply graphical editing to arrive at different presentations of the same data.

The concept of alternatives, which was introduced in the last example gives an additional justification for accumulation of the APL predicates in a skeleton. It allows to formulate the syntax for alternatives with one simple rule. The condition skeleton may also serve for overcoming space limitations. Long expressions or constant values may get a short name substitute. This is especially attractive if an expression appears several times.

The only language features which have not yet been shown are delete, insert, and update operations on tables and a macro facility, which could be used in the sense of tabular views. Macros provide means for customization of skeletons in addition to parametric queries. Macros are defined and saved like queries. They are never compiled, at compilation time they become substituted. This adds one additional object type, which is called VIEW, with the same binding rule as functions and three more keywords to designate a delete, insert and update row.

2.5.4 Summary

The query language encompasses a minimum of concepts, of commands, and of rules. Interactive usage with preferred sequences of commands is possible. Customization facilities allow to drop unwanted detail. Extension facilities can be used for proper modelling of specific application tasks. Differences of functions with regard to their implementation language are transparent at the query language level. The same transparency also applies to tables with regard to the underlying data base system. Consistency to APL can be maintained throughout. This allows to exploit any existing or developing APL skill for extension of the functional capabilities of the query language, with all the characteristics of learning APL. The query language is behaviorally extendable [THO74] and suitable for both, programmers and non-programmers. Little knowledge is required to begin with, users learn as much as they need and they learn it by doing (by example).

3. Managing the Application Knowledge

Application knowledge plays a central part in interactive problem solving. Not all aspects of application knowledge are fully under-stood yet and amenable to a systematization. What can be done is to build a guidance component, which provides on-line training and help facilities on usage of the system and the objects managed by the system. Of special importance is that additional layers can be intro-duced which may structure objects into meaningful groups over several levels. Whether the structure is designed top down or bottom up it can always be described by a set of nodes and a successor relation-ship between the nodes. Navigation through such an information network following the successor relationship supports hierarchical search.

The guidance component of IDAMS was designed for managing the appli-cation knowledge [ERB76], [ERB80]. The central part is a name vocab-ulary associated with information on the name usage. In addition to the already used object types TABLE, FUNCTION, QUERY, and VIEW (for the mentioned macro facility) there are some more objects needed to structure the system's facilities and its application knowledge. These are called EXTERNAL, APL, MENU, GUIDE, and TRAIN.

EXTERNAL covers information about non-APL functions embedded in attached program libraries. APL contains information on APL objects (functions and variable) which are used by IDAMS internally and/or by developed applications. MENU contains the data for panels used by IDAMS or by developed applications. GUIDE offers documentation facil-ities in form of a network, where the nodes carry information units, e. g., about objects and groups of objects. TRAIN is a self-contained learning-text collection, structured in tree-form which may be used to get familiar with the system.

3.1 Guidance Component Design Considerations

Functionally TRAIN and GUIDE could go together into one network, however, size considerations demand separation.

An automatic embedding into the guidance information network is provided by the name vocabulary with its associated usage information. The successor relationship for the different object types is managed by the name vocabulary services, transparent to the user. The name vocabulary supports quick answers to questions like

o show the names of all objects of a certain class
o show the classes which have an object with a certain name.

The realization of the simple idea of an information network gets complicated by the fact that names are not unique. There may be different objects with the same name belonging to the same or different object types. There may also evolve name conflicts between the developments of different users. The name vocabulary must provide means to handle such difficulties. It was considered intolerable to request that the user always fully qualifies the meaning of a name. The system must provide practicable defaulting. Three realizations of an object may exist with differences in ownership and lifetime. Lifetime gives the classification permanent versus temporary and ownership distinguishes between public and private. A temporary version will not exist beyond the current session. Having ten different object types and three possible realizations would allow for thirty different usages of a name. The priority rules that temporary overrules permanent and private overrules public simplify, since only conflicts between the different types must be resolved. Profiling provides a possible solution.

Profiling may be superimposed by associating a special mark to active objects. The role of profiling is twofold. It allows to resolve ambiguities if the same name is used for different objects. Even more important may be its possibility to restrict names to a smaller set, those objects which are important in the user's application context. The main advantage of profiling is that within the collection of active objects names have unique meaning. Despite its advantages profiling also introduces additional complexity. The user has to distinguish between active and non-active objects. It requires additional operations and transition rules.

Every enduser has complete freedom to introduce private objects, possibly with the intent to substitute public objects. However, he has no authority to change public objects. This is only allowed to

users with the system coordinator authority. The update authority is
also recorded in the user's profile.

The considerations for name defaulting will only be further elabo-
rated for the object type unit. Support of units is a unique feature
of IDAMS' query language. At table definition time table columns may
have a specified unit attached. The System will then check for proper
use of data in calculations (addition and subtraction is not allowed
for data with non-conformable units) and provide automatic conversion
of units where applicable. Conversion is done based on the compiler's
knowledge about units. Every known unit is expressed in terms of the
chosen basic units.   New units may be introduced by expressing them
in terms of already known units, e. g., km = m x 1000.

For consistency reasons the language rules for definition of units
are those of APL.   Any APL expression in terms of units and
constants, which evaluates to a meaningful unit is allowed. Within
the context of the query language the name restrictions implied by a
rich dictionary of units cannot be tolerated, therefore some additional mechanism is needed. The last one was chosen from the three
most obvious solution possibilities:
Prefix all unit names by a special character, e. g. a dollar sign;
add to every query definition the list of names meaning units;
use profiling to isolate the exploited unit names.

3.2 Functional Facilities of Guidance

The guidance component serves for selection, definition, and
description of objects. All kind of information is administrated,
formal definition as well as informal description. The information
may apply to objects, applications, or system usage.

Guidance supports HELP facilities, e. g. explanation of an item to
the name of which the cursor has been positioned followed by pushing
the PF1 key, and the analogous APL command
     HOW'<objectname>'.

The responsibility to care for description is attached to the SAVE
command. This is the latest point in time where services of the guidance component may be called for description of an object. The data
administration task of guidance includes services on the name vocabu-

lary (deletion, insertion, and renaming), but also much editor oriented work, e. g. change of stored texts.

Panels supporting selection processes are generated from information in the guidance component. Two different selection panels are supported, one with a linear arrangement of selectable items (normally in ascending sort order) the other with hierarchical grouping. The RUN command as applicable to every embedded function gets provided with formal definition and informal description through the guidance component.

3.3 Usability Considerations for Guidance

The value of the guidance component critically depends on the quality of the administrated text collections. Completeness and correctness are mandatory. Strict adherence to principles, which were layed down to allow, e. g., a uniform treatment of exceptional cases with meaningful messages is of major concern.

The best way to guarantee acceptance of such documentation discipline is to offer convenient services. Ease of use is important as well as reasonable defaulting. The documentation process must not start from an empty screen in general. Based on object definition the default offering for description may be a preformatted screen which indicates the proper layout and contains explanations what should or may go into individual sections.

The documentation discipline must adhere to simple mechanisms to avoid unmanageable complexity when the amount of information gets big. The data structures used to store text collections must support addition, deletion, and modification of objects. Transfer of private objects between two users is also required. Reorganization may occur occasionally, to improve the response by better clustering.

3.4 Training Component and Glossary

The training component consists of explanatory texts structured into roughly 50 groups. A group may fall into several smaller learning units, each fitting on one screen. The structure of the training system can be visualized by a tree:

```
GI............................... General information
  GUI.......................... General usage information
    GTH....................... General terminal handling
      TDF.................... Terminal display facilities
      TCP.................. Terminal cursor positioning
      TIC.................. Terminal input correction
    GSI...................... General system introduction
      SO.................... System objects
      SUG.................. System user guidance
  ...
```

The TRAIN facility will first display the hierarchical ordering of topics and the user may mark the topics he wants to see. The choice is for selected topics or for an entry to continuous training mode. A second selection facility is offered which presents the learning units in alphabetical order.

The screens belonging to one learning topic are shown together allowing to scroll up and down. Only part of the screen is used for display. A control block (top 3 lines) gives the short name, its explanation, and page information (XXX out of YYY). Screen layout is consistent with other usage.

The training is interruptible, and can also be resumed at the interrupted stage. This is of vital interest since train texts may describe examples and suggest problems to the user, which direct him to proper usage of the system facilities. He learns by example.

All information which belongs to the training component is stored in one external file. This makes isolation very simple and also allows easy conversion to a different national language.

An on-line glossary is supported by the same primitives. There is no segmentation into several screens per item and no hierarchical ordering between items used for the glossary. Display is either through the HOW '<item name>' command or by selection from a panel showing all glossary terms in alphabetical order, each term with a short explanation.

3.5 Information Network for Description

The primitives for the TRAIN offering can be extended to the more
general case of information networks. The objects themselves (each
represented by a node) form the basic node set. Various groupings may
be introduced as additional information nodes, each referencing the
names of its successor nodes. Nodes on the highest level (not refer-
enced by others) will be the candidates for the first selection panel
in a top down search process. Connections between nodes are specified
by attaching to each node the names of its successors. This seems to
require that names of nodes must be unique within an information
network. However, the System differentiates internally between names
of the different object classes. Therefore the guidance network does
not imply name restrictions between the different classes. As a
consequence in the specification of the names of successors it may
sometimes be required to use a class prefix to disambiguate, e. g.,
"F:" for Function, "T:" for Table.

Separation by ownership is also supported and by default private
overrules public. The system coordinator authority is required to
apply changes to public objects. The classification schema of the
name vocabulary automatically supports selection panels for all nodes
of one of the different types TABLE, UNIT, QUERY, FUNCTION, EXTERNAL,
VIEW, APL, MENU, GUIDE, or TRAIN. Further separation by ownership
and profile is also possible.

3.6 Embedding of New Applications

Application building corresponds to the choice step of interactive
problem solving. New applications may involve any of the available
objects of the system. In general they will be represented by a node
on the highest level in the guidance network. They may imply further
addition of new objects of any of the differentiated types. Control
of the resources used by an application part is kept in its guidance
information which records the names of "owned" objects exploiting the
successor relationship. Without such recording there is no way for
safe transfer of complete applications. All objects "owned" by an
application can be obtained by the transitive closure operation.

Saved queries automatically provide enough information. Other objects
which may be part of an application can easily be identified amongst

the private objects created during the application development cycle. Completion of the guidance for a new application can therefore be supported by a selection process on private objects. The structuring of necessary additional guidance nodes must be left to the discretion of the application experts.

4. Maintaining and Upgrading the System

The IDAMS-System cannot be maintained and upgraded without some programming skill. However, this only means that associated to a group of interactive non-programmer end users there must be a (programmer) system coordinator. In data base terminology it is the data base administrator. Design, creation and maintenance of data bases and application packages fall into his responsibility. As several new applications evolve it is the system coordinators task to verify that integration can be done without conflict. Of course he will already be participating during the design of new applications to avoid conflicting terminology, proposing e. g., naming rules and implementation strategies.

4.1 Integration of User Extensions

The principle that each user may have this private extension to the system needs the system coordinators decisions as to which objects should be kept from those of the private collections. He is also responsible for doing the needed changes, if any, in cooperation with the developers. To create a new version of the system he has to upgrade the system in turn by each extension individually.

The development of the IDAMS system was following exactly the same methodology. A new spin of the system was always created by integrating the various extensions during the last development cycle into the previous system spin. The set of extensions from different implementers needed stepwise verification. The new spin was developed doing the integration of one extension after the other, with verification that the implementer's version and the intermediate spin provided the same facilities. The new spin was ready after the last extension had become integrated and verified. From then on the new spin was used as base system.

For integration of new applications there may be the need not to put all applications into one system. Then several systems evolve, each requiring independent maintenance along the above described integration process.

4.2 Utilities Supporting Maintenance

IDAMS is not a small system. Its maintenance would have presented major problems without utilities, which were developed to do cross references and changes on-line, with system support. All systems information is kept on-line and therefore it is always up to date. This means that "guidance" was exploited already to build the system.

Only a few facilities will be mentioned: The call tree of functions may be shown including global and local usage of variables. Isolation of system parts may be accomplished by finding all global objects needed for a command. This is the transitive closure of an "owner"-relationship.

The principle of private extension applies to changes to the system. They are kept in external files without the need of workspace save. This provides isolation of changes and easy backout facilities, and also helps to save disk space.

Many of the IDAMS utilities directly contribute to the implementation of the guidance component, e. g. the call tree for functions and the hierarchical presentation of selection panels are supported by the same primitives. Many of the techniques used in building IDAMS can be exploited in building new applications. This applies to using the basic menu types and to using basic primitives as well.

5. Conclusion

The IDAMS system was developed as a research prototype. The implementation was not always along the groundrules layed down as
o minimal set of rules
o skeleton based high level non-procedural language
o maximally consistent interface design
o exploitation of display screens
o easy adaptation and extensibility

o predictability and comprehensiveness

o complexity appropriate to functional power

o easy translation into national language

A major drawback of the research prototype was the size caused by developing the system as an integration of already existing subsystems. This caused an unnecessary large working set and as a consequence, some response problems. Nevertheless some conclusions can be drawn from the joint studies performed.

5.1 Command and Menu Mode

The IDAMS interface evolved from a purely command driven version to a menu driven interface with facilities for command style usage. Our observations indicate, that frequent users of the menu interface always prefer the command style which is overlaid on the menu sequences, allowing to specify selections of successive menus in one move. Experienced users also prefer their own navigation. Therefore deep nesting of menus seems unattractive. Users get easily lost or feel uncomfortable.

Menu mode and command mode should best be combined providing very few basic menus, enough to get started easily, and building additional options into a command interface, combined with the menus, which allows experienced users to do their own navigation. Of course the system must back up such a command interface with the explanation of the currently allowed commands.

5.2 Minimize Complexity

A system as rich in functional capabilities as IDAMS may require much more awareness for good human factors. Functional complexity is frightening. Amazing enough: repetitions of simple steps shown altogether on a large screen create the impression of complexity.

Minimizing complexity therefore may mean to start from very simple applications, and to gradually refine and adapt the query language interface to evolving needs. Profiling has not the required quality. It is more inherent in the approach of structured programming. The interface of the system must be structured and adapted to the required tasks. This can probably be only achieved by associating enough programming expertise to the interactive problem solving group, that the customization actually takes place.

Acknowledgement

The current version of the Integrated Data Analysis and Management System has been built as a team work by R. ERBE, H. LEHMANN, G. MUEL-LER, and the author [SCH82]. Many colleagues at the Heidelberg Scientific Center have also contributed to IDAMS. The author would like to mention specifically A. Blaser, H. Eberle, and H. Schmutz, for their significant contributions. The contribution of R. Hartwig, J. Koehler, K. Mohr, and J. Redmer to graphical display facilities is also acknowledged.

References

CAS74 CARLSON, E.D., SUTTON, J.A.: A case Study of non-programmer Interactive Problem Solving. IBM Research Report RJ1382, April 1974

CHA76 CHAMBERLIN, D.: Relational Data Base Systems. Computing Surveys, Vol. 8 no. 1, 1976 pp. 43-66

CHN75 CHANG, C.L.: A hyper-relational model of databases. IBM Research Report RJ 1634, August 75

EBE77 EBERLE, H., SCHMUTZ, H.: Calling PL/1 or FORTRAN Subroutines dynamically from VS APL. IBM Scientific Center Technical Report TR 77.11.007

ERB76 ERBE, R., WALCH, G.: A General Interactive Guidance for Information Retrieval and Processing Systems. APL 76 (ed. G.T. Hunter), Ottawa 1976, pp. 127-140

ERB80 ERBE, R., HARTWIG, R., LEHMANN, H., MUELLER, G., SCHAUER, U.: Integrated Data Analysis and Management for the Problem Solving Environment. Information Systems Vol. 5, pp 273-285, Pergamon Press 1980

LOR74 LORIE, R.A.: XRM an Extended (n-ary) Relational Memory. IBM Technical Report 320-2096, January 1974

MUE83 MUELLER, G.: Endbenutzersysteme zur Entscheidungsunterstuetzung. Teubner-Verlag Stuttgart, 1983

RDS83 SCHMIDT, J.W., BRODIE, M.L.: Relational Database Systems. Analysis and Comparison. Springer Verlag Berlin Heidelberg New York, 1983

SCH82 SCHAUER, U., ERBE, R., LEHMANN, H., MUELLER, G.: Integrated Data Analysis and Management System. DSS-82 Transactions (ed. G.W. Dickson) San Francisco 1982, pp.

THO74 THOMAS, J. C., GOULD, J.D.: A psychological study of Query Example. IBM Research Report RC 5124, November 1974

ZLO74 ZLOOF, M.M.: Query by Example. IBM Research Report RC 4917, July 1974

HUMAN FACTORS OF A 'NATURAL LANGUAGE' ENDUSER SYSTEM

Magdalena Zoeppritz
IBM Germany
Heidelberg Scientific Center
Tiergartenstrasse 15
D-6900 Heidelberg

1 INTRODUCTION

The idea of communicating with a computer in natural language has stimulated the imagination for quite some time and has given rise to a debate about the advantages and disadvantages this might have. Some of this discussion is carried out on a more philosophical plane, some of it is derived from experimentation with different kinds of simulated situations, but very little of it is based on experience with implemented natural language systems.

Given that the interaction language of a system is important for its human factors, it is easy for those who think that even restricted natural language is useful for data analysis, as we did and still do, to believe that a natural language interface to a relational data base will have good human factors by definition, and in proportion to the natural language syntax and semantics implemented in it. The system we built on these premises is User Specialty Languages (USL, cf. references under Lehmann, Ott, and Zoeppritz). Of course, we have found out in the meantime that even natural language systems must tell about errors politely, need some training, hence a legible manual, and can be just as frustrating as any other system when the diagnostics are not sufficiently clear.

On the other hand, our system has had several users who had data they wanted to analyze and who let us study how they used the system. At first, this was only intended to detect functional and linguistic errors, constructions that were needed and we had not thought about, interpretations that were inconsistent with other people's usage, etc., and to find out in general whether natural language was feasible with the restrictions imposed by our system. But the

studies with users also offered an opportunity to observe natural
language communication with a computer, with respect to functional
requirements (do they use pronouns and if so for what purpose?) and
with respect to user attitudes and strategies (how do they formulate
their questions and what happens if there is an error?).

There is not very much data about the use of natural language with
implemented systems (but see Woods et al., 1972, Damerau, 1979, and
Tennant, 1979). The purpose of this paper is to contribute to the
discussion about the desirability of communicating with computers in
natural language by comparing some of the statements for and against
natural language with what we observed in our studies with users.
The first section describes the features of the system which are
relevant for the argument, leaving out technical detail. The second
section gives an overview of the studies. Then, in the third
section, some of the arguments for and against natural language are
presented and discussed.

2 THE USER SPECIALTY LANGUAGES SYSTEM

2.1 PROPERTIES OF THE SYSTEM

The User Specialty Languages System (USL) is designed as an
applications independent natural language interface to a relational
data base for data query, analysis, and manipulation, including data
entry. The underlying data base management system now is System R
(Chamberlin et al., 1981), earlier versions of USL interfaced to the
Peterlee Relational Test Vehicle (Todd, 1975). USL analyzes and
interprets natural language sentences. From the interpretation, the
system generates one or several expressions in the formal data base
query language. This language was Information Systems Base Language
(ISBL) for the Peterlee Relational Test Vehicle (PRTV), it now is
Structured Query Language (SQL) for communication with System R.

The project started out as a joint effort to construct interfaces for
several natural languages using the same technology. The basic
concepts of the technology derive from the Rapidly Extensible
Language (REL) System of Thompson et al.(1969). While both the
present REL System (cf. Henisz-Thompson 1978) and the USL System

differ in important respects from one another and from the technology
of REL in 1969, three basic principles have remained:

1. Ambiguous sentences lead to more than one interpretation.
2. Syntactic rules are accociated with semantic interpretations and
3. Applictions independent elements of the language are built into
   the system, applications dependent material is added by the user.

The parser accepts general phrase structure grammars, it is User
Language Generator (Bertrand et al., 1981) and derived from the Kay
parser (Kay, 1967), but with considerable extensions and
modifications. The grammar rules each contain the name of the
interpretation routine which represents the meaning of the
construction analyzed by the rule. The parser works through the
input right to left, bottom up, producing all parses in parallel.
Ambiguous sentences lead to several trees spanning the input. For
full parses, the interpretation routines accociated with the nodes in
the tree are called, starting at the root of the tree. The
parameters of the interpretation routines are <u>not</u> resolved locally.

Applications independence in USL, as in REL, rests on distinguishing
in natural language between features that have the same form and
function irrespective of subject matter and those that do not. Among
the first are syntactic constructions and structural words, among the
latter are most nouns, verbs, adjectives, and proper names.

The nouns, verbs, and adjectives that users need for their
application are entered by the users themselves via a prompting
routine. Each user defined noun, verb, or adjective addresses a
relation in the data base. For these relations, USL assumes a view
of data that is close to natural language: The columns of these
relations each have one of the following five data types:

Name of type	Values	Example
WORD	Proper name	employee <u>Meier</u>
CODE	Coded name	part <u>4326,</u>
NUMBER	Measure/amount	salary <u>2345,</u>
QUANTITY	Counted number	population <u>2345,</u>
DATE	Time data	meeting on <u>Monday</u>

Each column also has one of a set of standard role-names. These role-names correspond to the way in which the underlying concepts are interrelated, as reflected in the way that the words are used in the user's application jargon. For example a relation ADDRESS could be defined in the following ways, depending on purpose and data of the application (role-names are capitalized, the list is not meant to be exhaustive):

```
Two columns:     NOM_address  OF_person
Three columns:   NOM_Address  OF_person AT_time
Four columns:    NOM_Address  OF_person FROM_date TO_date
Five columns:    NOM_Address  OF_person IN_town FROM_date TO_date
```

Details on data types and role-names are found in Lehmann et al. (1977 and forthcoming), Quantity was introduced in Zoeppritz (1979), criticism of Zoeppritz (1979) is found in Krause (1982).

Having the relations for USL physically stored would lead in large data bases to duplication of information, update problems, and problems with application programs. Therefore the relations are defined as views on data base relations with a different structure. The translation from queries against views to queries against the base relations is done by the viewoptimizer program (Ott and Horländer 1982).

2.2 APPLICATIONS INDEPENDENCE

The fact that the system does not rely on a specific data base and specific vocabulary makes its generalizations truly applications independent. Though solutions to problems of natural language analysis are sought for the general case also in many systems designed for a specific application domain, the interpretation in these systems uses information that has to be obtained separately for each data base and that may not necessarily be within the power of unsophisticated users to supply consistently and in accordance with the system's understanding of the information. With this information, however, the analysis can in principle be more subtle and the responses more natural than they can be within the framework of USL.

2.3 ANALYSIS AND INTERPETATION

The following information is obtained from the user and used in the
analysis and interpretation:
1. The name, role names, and data types of the views he has defined
   on the relations in his data base for his vocabulary.
2. The vocabulary of the application with the wordclass and some
   morphological information for each vocabulary item.

The analysis proceeds in five steps, which shall be only briefly
outlined here. Details of the syntactic analysis, step one, are
found in Zoeppritz (manuscript). The interpretation, steps two to
four, will be described in Lehmann and Ott (forthcoming), view
optimization is described in Ott and Horländer (1982).

Syntactic analysis yields one or more trees spanning the sentence
that was entered. Each node in the tree is associated with the name
of the interpretation routine that was specified in the rule
according to which the node has been constructed.

In a second step, the invoking program calls, separately for each
tree, the interpretation routines found for that tree from the top
down. The interpretation routines are programs written in PL/I. The
interpretation routines successively build relational structures
which contain the values and relation names found in the query,
related to one another according to the functional dependencies
expressed in the syntactic structures of the sentence.   Apart from
generating the relational structure, the interpretation routines pick
up or generate, and store, semantic information for later use. The
routines called for nounphrases, for instance, also calculate a
referent variable from gender and number of the underlying noun.
This information is used if a possessive pronoun is present in the
sentence.   In the same way, the points where negatives,
interrogatives, quantifiers, or coordinated structures occur are
found and remembered until all substructures are processed and
related.

In a third step, the relational structure resulting from the
interpretation routines found in the tree is marked with regard to
scope of quantifiers, interrogatives, negation, and coordination.
The procedure is complicated if several quantifiers cooccur and

interact with negation and coordination. Details of the solutions to scope problems are found in Lehmann (1978a) and Lehmann and Ott (forthcoming).

The fourth step contains the generation of SQL queries from the relational structure, using the information evaluated in the third step for decisions as to where subqueries, multiple queries, or intersections of multiple queries are to be generated.

The resulting SQL query or queries are transmitted to the viewoptimizer. The viewoptimizer replaces the SQL query generated so far, which addresses the data base through the views defined for USL, by a query in terms of the base relations and their columns.

The SQL string transformed by the viewoptimizer is sent to the data base management system. The resulting answer is either directly transmitted to the user terminal or it is transformed by USL before transmission to the user, primarily in the case of yes/no questions and some types of coordinated sentences.

2.4 SUMMARY OF PROPERTIES AFFECTING THE USER

1. Though there is disambiguation at every step of the analysis and code generation, truly ambiguous input will result in several analyses. So users are confronted with ambiguity. On the other hand, there is less chance that the analysis done is not the one intended.

2. The vocabulary needed by the user for his data must be entered by the user himself or by somebody else for him and in close contact with him. This is not difficult, but not altogether easy, particularly if a given word is to be used in several ways. Furthermore, the menus for defining vocabulary are better at getting morphological information and the kind of objects and adverbials used than they are at asking for adverbials in the first place. Since vocabulary and view definitions must match, this connection should be made explicit in the definition routine. Now the menues ask questions like: 'are you using this word with time specifications?' without answering the obvious question 'Why would I want to do that', i. e. linking the questions about use of words to the views he has defined in the data base. Since

users define their own views, they know about the connection. The
way the questions are put now, users may either feel at liberty to
change their minds about the definitions (which they can do, but
not via this routine), or they may feel that the system is hiding
something from them. We have not found out yet how to put that
into the menu in a reasonable way.

3. There is not more application specific semantics than the users
   provide themselves. The system will not know that employees are
   people, unless people are defined as the union of employees,
   pensioners, etc. On the other hand, the system does not penalize
   users for asking for the salary of Jim's house, if they so choose,
   other than not having data on this subject.

4. The structure of views on the relations in the database must be
   built. This structure mediates between the linguistic side of the
   system and a database that may be used for other purposes than
   query in natural language. In this way, the natural language
   interface does not disrupt the data base structure. However, the
   definition of views requires asking oneself 'How am I talking
   about this data'. This is not quite as easy as we had thought it
   would be, but it turns out to be slightly easier for naive users
   than for people trained in data base design and systems analysis.

3 APPLICATIONS

The data presented here is based on the protocols of five
applications with 8589 interactions altogether. The protocols were
obtained by spooling the screen image onto a console file. They
record all interactions with the system, user input, system
responses, and, by number of blips or empty lines, wait times. In
addition we have solicited and unsolicited comments from the users.
Applications and results are described for the application Grades in
Krause (1979, 1980b, 1982), Lehmann and Krause (1979), and Ott
(1979a). The early applications are the basis of Lehmann et al.
(1978). The Rooms application is described in Kettler et al. (1981),
with a comparison of the implementations of the application in User
Specialty Languages and the BEAST system (Habel et al, 1977). The
following two tables shall give some figures on number of relations,
size of the vocabulary, number of users and interactions, time and

duration of use, and number of errors related to number of questions. The error rate given refers to <u>any</u> 'misunderstanding' between user and system, including obvious user errors like typing errors, missing definitions, etc. Detailed error analyses were done for the Grades (Krause, 1982) and Rooms (Kettler et al. 1981) applications.

Table 1: Overview of the structure of applications

Application	Relations		Nouns	Adjectives	Verbs	Names
	Base	Virtual				
Planning	3	71	148	4	4	1
Reception	6	50	55	6	29	0
History	2	38	41	6	0	0
Rooms	4	105	109	19	12	173
Grades	6	79	91	2	9	1

Table 2: Overview of the use of the system

Application	Duration	Users	Questions	%Errors
Planning	May 76 - October 76	2	59	46.0
Reception	February 77	1	115	47.0
History	December 76 - April 77	1	356	12,9
Rooms	February 78 - March 79	3	781	39.9
Grades	February 78 - October 79	3	7278	8.1
Total		10	8589	

For results of these studies, see Lehmann et al. (1978), Kettler et al. (1981), and Krause (1979, 1982).

The time needed for defining relations, views, and vocabulary for an application varied from two weeks (History) to three months (Grades), the latter included entering the data from manually kept class books. In all other cases the data was available in machine readable form.

Two applications were done with the English version of the system, one with the International Institute of Applied Systems Analysis, the other with New York University. The study planned with IIASA did not materialize for nontechnical reasons. The second application and first results from it are described in Turner et al. (1982). Comparisons of USL and formal languages were done with different designs by Krause (1982), Purnadi (1981), and Turner et al. (1982).

The content of the applications was as follows:

Planning involved data on installations and marketing of machines. This very early application was a major source for extensions to our system.

Reception wanted a facility for people at the reception desk that would help them bring visitors into contact with the people in charge of fields of interest to the visitors. The data were names, telephone numbers, areas of interest, offices etc.

History was done by a school interested in background, schooling, and examinations of their students prior to a study of their careers after school.

Rooms was done with the administration of the Technical University of Berlin, who wanted to control the allocation of rooms and office space on-line, and with the Computer Science Department of the Technical University of Berlin, who wanted to compare USL with BEAST (Habel et al. 1977).

Grades was done with another school, the Karl Friedrich Gymnasium, Mannheim. The goal was to find out whether the grades at the end of the fifth year of school can predict success in the final exam after the thirteenth year.

4 DISCUSSION OF ARGUMENTS

The discussion about the desirability of using natural language for communicating with a computer has been both long and heated (cf. Sammet, 1969, Hill, 1972, Montgomery, 1972). The arguments range from 'the ultimate non-procedural language is natural language' (Pierotte, 1978:41) to 'typical users may not be aware of the semantics of question asking' (Shneiderman, 1978:428). Lehmann and Blaser (1979) point out that much of the discussion is speculative in nature, and must remain so as long as so few of the natural language systems have been tested in field situations, with users analyzing their own data. I shall not try to list all the arguments (this is done in Lehmann and Blaser, 1979) or trace the history of the discussion (but see Krause, 1982, and Turner et al., 1982). This section shall present some of these arguments and compare them with the data we collected from the users of our system. The following arguments shall be discussed:

For natural language:

1. 'Man already knows his natural language and if he is to use a computer seldom or as a minor part of his work, then he may not have the time or inclination to learn a formal machine language' (Woods et al., 1972:1.2).

2. 'English is therefore an attractive medium because the human can express his ideas in the form in which they occur to him' (Woods et al., 1972:1.2).

3. 'Complex facts can be expressed also by inexperienced users of a system, because natural language provides powerful syntactic tools' (Habel et al. 1977:3, my translation).

4. 'It drastically reduces for the occasional user the psychological barrier against using a computer that is caused by his or her having to learn an artificial language' (Habel et al. 1977:3, my translation).

Against natural language:

1. 'Any natural (language) system in the foreseeable future is likely to place serious restrictions on the vocabulary and syntax of allowable, or at least useful user inputs to the system. It may be difficult for the user to keep in mind such restrictions since daily conversation may tend to provide strong interference with the rules of such a system' (Thomas and Gould, 1975:439).

2. 'For (natural language front ends), natural language may provide no benefit beyond a slightly easier learning task for the new operators, and has the cost of requiring more words or characters to be typed to get something done' (Woods, 1977:20).

3. 'Typical users may not be aware of the semantics of question asking' (Shneiderman, 1978:428).

4. 'English is really far too wooly and ambiguous to do the job well' (Hill, 1972:306).

5. 'Natural human communication is characterized by a great many small errors that would result in a complete failure of communication between man and computer' (Chapanis, 1973:215).

6. '(Users attempt) to request information which is not contained in the data base' (Shneiderman, 1978:427-428).

In the following sections I shall address counterargument 1 under Restrictions, and arguments and counterarguments 2 to 4 under Wordiness. Then counterarguments 5 and 6 are discussed in sequence, followed by argument 1, Training. Examples shall be given in English, unless the problem is language specific. Excerpts from protocols are given in German with English glosses.

4.1 DIGRESSION: PROCEDURAL VS DESCRIPTIVE

In the discussion about natural language communication with computers, natural language has often been treated as a homogeneous whole, styles and modes have been disregarded. As several authors have found (a. o. Lehmann and Blaser, 1979), arguments originally voiced against natural language programming are now also used in discussions about natural language query. That the properties of descriptive and procedural query languages differ considerably seems to be obvious. That giving instructions and asking questions are different modes of using natural language with different properties, is largely overlooked, though everyone knows from experience that giving directions on how to operate a washing machine is a different type of task from asking about the voltage at which it operates.

Similarly, when we talk about 'good' instructions, we are saying that they were succesful in helping us to accomplish the task. When we talk about 'good' questions, we usually mean that somebody thought about something interesting to ask, but we do not comment on how the question was put. We usually take for granted that people manage to express what they want to know, we do not in the same way take for granted that people give instructions without overlooking something or getting the sequence mixed up.

For this reason I would like to emphasize that our observations about natural language communication with a computer were made with a system with restricted natural language for data base access. The users were native speakers of German and used the German version of the system. Input to the system was by typing at the keyboard. Some of the users were programmers (Planning and Reception), most of them were not. They were professionals in the sense that they had collected the data for the purposes of their work and knew what data was available, though not necessarily the form in which it was stored. With the exception of the Grades application, they had developed a jargon in which to speak about the data before using USL. The Grades group developed their jargon as they were building the data base from manually kept classbooks. They were not casual users. With the exception of the user who built the Reception application, they were occasional users in that 1 to 14 days intervened between sessions. This is the context in which the observations were made, they need not apply to other kinds of tasks and other types of users.

4.2 RESTRICTIONS

4.2.1 Effect of restrictions: syntax and semantics

The syntactic and semantic capabilities of the USL system were fully used, but there were differences in frequency. Thus, the users of the History application frequently used appositions, e.g. occupationgroup 5 (293 in 356 queries), while appositions do not occur at all in the first 95 questions of the Grades application. We have not done structure counts for the other applications and for the bulk of the questions in the Grades application, but from looking at the protocols, great differences in the frequencies of structures seem to be the normal case. The occurrence or non-occurrence of a construction in a given application, then, does not say much about the need for the construction in general. More important seems to be the place that a given construction has in the linguistic system. According to Krause (1982), who studied the Grades application in depth, it is the purely syntactic gaps that are most difficult for users to avoid (and they should not have to). By syntactic gaps we mean missing structural variants of constructions that are within the limits of what the system can handle semantically. The following example from Krause (1982:138 and Appendix) shall illustrate this: One of the users regularly placed the adverbial after the participle.

Wieviele Schüler sind nichtversetzt in Sexta
How many students are not promoted in class5

The syntax at that time only had a rule for adverbial before participle:

Wieviele Schüler sind in Sexta nichtversetzt
How many students are in class5 not promoted

Even though the user knew in principle that the first wording would not be understood by the system, he used it all the time. So we believe that it is not useful to restrict syntactic variation.

Since in most cases rules were added relatively soon after such omissions were discovered - one purpose of the studies was, after all, to make the system less dependent on the language of the developers - there are not many examples for long term irritation caused by syntactic gaps. After the gaps are closed, it is difficult to assess the weight of the corresponding changes for the sessions that follow. Syntax is a dissatisfier!

According to Krause (1982), semantic restrictions are easy to accept where they concern an entire semantic complex. Users had no difficulty accepting, for example, that the system could not answer why questions. Also, at the time of the History application, the user had no difficulty avoiding questions that ask for subtotals, like How many students have which exam, after he found out that the system could not do them. What is interesting in the last example is that, contrary to why questions, the subtotalling function was essential to this and other users and they missed it badly (it was implemented soon after). One would have expected that users would address the function inadvertently, just like the adverbial was inadvertently put after the participle. That this did not happen we relate to the fact that syntactic behavior is much less consciously controlled than is semantic behavior.

An interesting intermediate type of restriction appears where a given
syntactic construction has different semantic interpretations,
depending on its elements, as in the following example with <u>more than</u>

```
Who earns more than 5000      compare numbers
Who earns more than Paul      find salary of Paul
                              then compare numbers
```

If one of the interpretations is implemented and the other is not,
the resulting gaps are semantic gaps as regards the system. From the
user's point of view, because the same syntactic construction is
involved, these omissions have the same effect as syntactic gaps and
are as difficult to avoid. Corresponding errors were frequent and
were made even by us, the system developers, who in principle knew
very well how far a new construction was implemented. Conversely, it
happened several times that errors occurring with a newly implemented
construction showed us that the construction was not as semantically
homogeneous as the syntactic form had led us to believe.

From the studies we can say that restrictions of natural language are
the more easy to accept the more consciously the corresponding
linguistic faculties are handled by people. People are less
conscious of details of word order and subtle differences of meaning
within constructions than they are of words and semantic fields.
Consequently, given the required function, restrictions of the
semantics and of the syntactic variantion of constructions that are
in principle available in the system cause more difficulties than
things altogether left out.

4.2.2 Effect of restrictions: Meaning of words

It is intuitively clear that a relation like 'subject-of' is constant
in function and potentially represented by the same set of syntactic
configurations in all thematic contexts, though some configurations
may be preferred for pragmatic reasons. The same holds for
prepositions, conjunctions, and pronouns. The distinction between
subject matter dependent and independent meanings and functions of
nouns, verbs, and adjectives needs some comment. Relatively clear
cases are the words for months and weekdays or for units of measure.
Though some of these words are also used as proper names, it can
hardly be said that the meaning of e. g. <u>Friday</u> varies between name

of day and proper name according to subject matter, but rather that there are two names <u>Friday,</u> one denoting a specific day of the week, the other referring to a person in some contexts.

For the verbs <u>to be</u> and <u>to have,</u> the copula and associative aspects of meaning can be separated from the existential end possessive meanings respectively (cf. Bach 1967:476-477). The former remain constant over different contexts, the latter are actualized in specific contexts.

But also for words like <u>house, life, person</u> it could be argued that their meaning does not vary to the same extent as the well known examples <u>bank</u> or <u>batter.</u> It is there that the distinction made in USL becomes significant in that even words like <u>house, life,</u> and <u>person</u> are not part of the system and are not present in the vocabulary, unless they have been defined by a user for his or her data base. This means that the user is not confronted with general meanings of words that have a very specific meaning in the context of his data base. A user talking about weather reports may not want to have to constantly avoid being misunderstood, because <u>shower</u> can also mean <u>shower for the bride, shower in the bathroom,</u> to give just two examples of terms for which <u>shower</u> is used in different jargons without further specification, because the specific meaning is given by the subject matter.

USL contains a basic vocabulary of about 450 words, consisting mainly of prepositions, conjunctions, articles, and pronouns. The vocabulary also includes units of measure, names of days and months, arithmetic operators, and the verbs <u>to have</u> and <u>to be</u> . The meanings of these words are represented in the system. While this is quite satisfactory for structural words like prepositions and articles, there are difficulties with some nouns and verbs, where the system definition does not reflect extensions of meaning. In many cases this also involves going beyond what can be answered from a data base, as illustrated by the following examples:

What is the average life expectancy of carpenters?
Where does the average carpenter live?

Not all the aspects of meaning that are left out can be written off as 'metaphorical'. There are quite natural transitions between the

literal meaning of <u>average</u> with numbers and just as literal meanings
of <u>average</u> with people.

All other vocabulary is added by the user. He can enter nouns, verbs,
adjectives, and names that are relevant in connection with his data
base. Names need only be entered in special cases, since the system
interprets all unknown words as names. User vocabulary is connected
by the user to the relations (or views) in his data base.   It can
also be connected to an operation performed by an interpretation
routine written by the user. This is not a trivial task and has not
been done so far.

Restricting the meaning of a word in this way to the relation it
addresses, specifically the set of values in the NOM-column of that
relation, has a similar effect of leaving out aspects of meaning that
users will actualize without at first being aware of a transition.

     How big is the floorspace of room 204
     Which is the biggest room

As can be seen from the first question, <u>room</u> refers to a set of room
numbers, a second relation <u>floorspace</u> contains the floor space for
each room. However it is quite natural to ask for the largest room,
as regards size, without mentioning size.   The problem is known as
the problem of intervening relations, a solution has been proposed
that depends on intellectually anticipating and weighting columns
that are likely to appear in joins, given a specific data base (Chang
1978), but there does not seem to be a general solution.

Most users did not have any difficulty with these restrictions, if
they encountered them at all, but some users did and intervening
relations remain a problem.

4.2.3 Effect of restrictions: Size of vocabulary

This relates to another question: If users know what data is
available, will they require all words in the language that are used
to refer to these data items, which would make even application
dependent vocabularies rather large, or can and will they restrict
themselves. Vocabularies in USL applications varied from 47 to 313
words. Of the 313, 173 were defined names so that rooms could be

identified by their nicknames instead of the cumbersome identification code. With the general vocabulary of about 450 words (prepositions, articles, temporals, arithmetic and aggregate operators, etc.) from about 500 to about 750 words were available. Since the users could define more words if they needed them, or have us define them, we can assume that the number of words in a given application was sufficient for the purposes of that application.

That agrees with the results of Kelly and Chapanis (1977) and Michaelis et al. (1977), who conclude that people can adapt to restricted vocabularies. The most restricted group in Michaelis et al. (1977) has 300 words, 225 general and 75 problem specific. In their conclusion, they suggest that even smaller vocabularies could have been used. They point out, however, that small vocabularies must be carefully tailored to the application if users shall work with them successfully.

For an applications independent system, this would mean that the general vocabulary is not the place where restrictions should be made, but that adding a relatively small number of words for a specific application may be sufficient for an individual or group to successfully analyze their data.

The figures from USL and Michaelis et al. (1977) are comparable by the order of magnitude, but not in detail, because of the following differences: The figure of 450 given for the general vocabulary in USL counts different forms of the same word as one word, Michalis et al. (1977) count them as different words. This way, the general vocabulary in USL would come to be about 750 for German. Also, the general vocabulary in Michaelis et al. (1977) includes words that would be part of the application in USL, e. g. equipment, but several of the words in the general vocabulary of USL are left out in Michaelis' 225, notably how and many. The restrictions in Michaelis et al. (1977) are placed not only on the application specific vocabulary, but also on the general vocabulary. In the interest of applications independence, the restrictions in USL are much less severe. Imagine a system where it is not possible to use how many in any application. On the other hand, much of the general vocabulary is not used in a given application: there may not be any time data, hence no use of temporals except maybe requests for today's date. Or none of the words defined for the application governs the preposition about, so this preposition is not used. This is similar to how syntactic constructions were used.

4.3 WORDINESS

4.3.1 Too much typing

The statement by Woods (1977:20) in which he referred to restricted natural language front ends as 'requiring more words or characters to be typed to get something done', has been generally accepted and is often used to explain why natural language systems need not be considered. So in Gaines (1981:134) 'The typing required by the user to generate complete English sentences is too great'. This argument is taken up in Krause (1982). He compared the lengths of queries in a relatively concise formal language (ISBL, Todd, 1975), with the corresponding natural language queries. Krause used the natural language questions from one terminal session of one user of the Grades application (90 questions). These questions were given to subjects experienced both in ISBL and in the application to put to the system in ISBL. Experienced subjects were chosen to get the best possible formulation in the formal language. Though most operators of ISBL consist of only one symbol, the lenghths are about equal (for details, see Krause, 1982:246-247). For half of the 20 sentence patterns, at least one of the formal expressions chosen is longer. Where the formal expressions are shorter, the difference is one or two characters.

Comparison with SQL looks rather worse for the formal language, because the operators in SQL are entire words. Two examples shall illustrate this:

    Which employee lives in Heidelberg

    SELECT UNIQUE EMPLOYEE
           FROM EMP
           WHERE TOWN = 'HEIDELBERG'

Which employee does not live in Heidelberg

```
SELECT UNIQUE X EMPLOYEE
      FROM EMP X
      WHERE X.EMPLOYEE NOT IN
        (SELECT UNIQUE Y.EMPLOYEE
              FROM EMP
              WHERE Y.TOWN='HEIDELBERG')
```

Obviously, abbreviations for the names of relations and columns would have made the formal expressions shorter, but still not shorter than their natural language equivalents, and abbreviations can also be used in natural language. So natural language does not mean more typing.

4.3.2 Wordiness vs complex operators

The two examples above show another property of natural language. If natural language is called wordy and not as concise as a formal language, the power of natural language 'operators', of words like no or not, or of syntactic relations like subject or object is often overlooked. Lehmann and Blaser (1979) point out that the users of USL did not start with simple questions and used more complicated ones later on, but that they asked complex questions right from the start, complex in the sense that they required joins and grouping operations in the data base. In formal languages, such operators are often taught late and can be difficult to learn and use (Reisner, 1977).

Mastering the syntax of a formal language and the semantics of its operators is only part of the problem of learning a formal language. The more important part, as I see it, is for the user to be able to judge, when he has formulated a complex expression, whether the expression corresponds semantically to what he actually wants to know. As a result, there is such a thing as 'debugging' for formal queries.

Shneiderman (1981:126) addresses this problem as follows: 'I conjecture that experienced query language users compose queries by building an internal semantic structure which is language independent and then interpret their queries into the syntax of the target language'. This interpretation process would also involve what he calls 'decomposition into lower level semantic knowledge', i. e. for the user to translate the internal semantic structure of what he wants to know into the lower level semantics of the target language. The confidence with which users can translate will affect what they can ask.

In their study of Query by Example (Zloof, 1974), Thomas and Gould (1975:441) asked their subjects (trained but not experienced) to translate English questions into Query by Example. They also asked them to give a confidence rating betwen 1 (very sure correct) and 5 (very sure incorrect) to indicate how sure they were that each query was correct. They report a mean confidence rating of 1.8 (s.d.=0.82). While the subjects were slightly more than 'fairly sure' that their queries were correct, they were not all absolutely sure.

That natural language users are sure that their questions are correct and mean what they want to say became obvious whenever the system reacted in an unexpected manner. The users did not question their own use of the language but complained about the syntax and semantics of the system. A 'syntax error' or an incorrect answer was the system's error, not theirs.

If one assumes that people will not formulate questions the meaning of which is not clear to them, any language has the effect of reducing the information people can request to what they can express with confidence in the language they use. This sounds trivial, but the consequences are not.

It seems plausible to assume, as Woods et al. (1972) do, that users formulate their questions in natural language as they occur to them, while otherwise they may be restricted by their knowledge of the formal language. Since even rather innocent looking natural language expressions are often the equivalents of rather complicated formal expressions, the limits of what users can ask are moved further out.

4.3.3 Complex operators: Pronouns

When we postponed implementing possessives, demonstratives, and personal pronouns, we knew that this restriction would make the system less natural. We suspected, but had no proof, that we were thereby restricting function. We assumed that most of the function of these wordclasses would be available through variable definition:

    who lives in Heidelberg   aaa=people living in Heidelberg
    what is their address   what is aaa's address

The following examples proved for us that pronouns are more than 'nice to have' (I have changed the application jargon for the first example):

    y=Zahlungen der Kunden, deren Schulden größer als
    ihre Zahlungen sind
    y=payments of customers whose amounts due are greater than
    their payments

    Wieviele nichtversetzte Schüler in Sexta haben Deutschnote 2
    in dieser Sexta
    How many nonpromoted students in class5 have Germangrade 2
    in this class5

    Wieviele Schüler haben Deutschnote 2 in Sexta und sind in ihr
    nichtversetzt?
    How many students have Germangrade 2 in class5 and were
    not promoted in it

The second and third examples are taken from Krause (1982:203-4). There were four classes 5, and nonpromoted students had been in two of them.

In all three cases, the pronoun or demonstrative requires an additional match between the customer who pays and the customer who owes and between class of nonpromotion and class in which the grade was given to make them the same customer or class. This match cannot be achieved by set operations on defined variables. In the Grades case, the only way to avoid pronouns turned out to be to ask for the individual classes by name, as in 'How many students who are not promoted in K501 have Gemangrade 2 in K501'. That was feasible, because there were only four of them, but in the general case it obviously is not.

4.3.4 Complex operators: A note on quantification

Problems with the use and interpretation of quantifiers by users have been pointed out several times. A detailed study by Thomas (1976) describes several difficulties. The main problem seems to be that logicians and users of natural language do not agree among themselves and with logicians. I shall compare some our results with his. All examples are translated.

Thomas (1976:12) reports the impression of two data base managers that complex queries involving (in the context: universal) quantifiers were rarely used. In our studies, all in the sense of the universal quantifier was also rarely used. It occurred once in the 781 questions of the Rooms application, 6 times in the 7278 questions of Grades, and not at all in the other applications. The question from Rooms was: Do all buildings have at least 30 rooms? The way that this question is formulated suggests that it was not a use question, but a test question, to see whether quantifiers worked. In Grades, the questions were of the form Are all variable1 variable2, and served the purpose of checking the consistency of definitions.

Use of all to ask for an exhaustive list (redundantly, since the system did not select), occurred more often than use of all in the sense of the universal quantifier. It occurred in 15 out of 59 questions in the Planning application and in 12 out of 781 questions of the Rooms application. It was used by nonprogrammers and programmers. Our suggestion is that hypercorrectness and computerese may play a role.

The most frequently used quantifier was the interrogative how many, numerical quantifiers follow at a distance, most often in the form more than 2 rooms, less than 5 classes. Exact numbers sometimes occurred for consistency checks: Wieviele Schüler sind nichtversetzt in 2 Quarten (they should match the number of repeaters).

Thomas (1976:15) observed strategies to get information without having to use quantifiers. Such strategies are:

1. Asking a sequence of questions
2. Defining (and intersecting) variables

2. Using negative existential instead of universal quantifier
   'Are there any that do not' instead of 'do all'
3. Sequence of questions to home in on whether 'all A are B' means subset or equivalence.
4. He points out that people often prefer qualification rather than quantification
   'Put the red block in the box'
   rather than 'if a block is red, put it in the box'

All these structures were used in the studies, not necessarily to avoid quantification, more in the sense of his second recommendation: It was possible for users to gather information in ways that are consistent with their natural strategies (Thomas, 1976:16).

Thomas notes that there is a general assumption that natural language systems ought to interpret quantifiers, but that, according to his findings, universal quantification in the logical sense may not be as important as has been assumed. For universal quantification, the frequency of 7 in 8589 questions seems to point in the same direction. On the other hand, frequency of occurrence usually does not show how badly something will be missed if it is not there. Consistency checking turned out to be a major step in data base set up, serving to locate errors in the original data. For other quantifiers, the counts we made indicate that, even though the frequencies for quantifiers except <u>wieviel</u> were not very high, numeric quantification seems to be important. In view of the use of <u>all</u> as equivalent of the definite article, it is useful to follow Thomas in not expecting only the logician's view of how they should be used.

4.4 ERRORS IN THE INPUT

Chapanis (1973) observed ungrammatical sentences in an experiment investigating communication between people, mostly in <u>spoken</u> language. A recent study (Zoltan et al., 1982) references several experiments where people communicated with other people or people with computer programs (some simulated) by writing or by voice. Zoltan et al. found that generally a much higher number of errors (mispronounciation, misspelling, ungrammatical utterances, etc.) was reported for experiments where people had communicated with people than it was where people communicated with a computer. Zoltan et al. interpret these findings as suggesting that results from interpersonal communication may not in all cases also apply to communication with a computer. In their own study, they pursued this question. The subjects were asked to manage their checking accounts with the help of a computer program, one group by typing at the keyboard, another group by voice. They conclude: 'Subjects in our study made fewer typographical errors and spelling errors in the keyboard condition and fewer stutters and false starts in the voice condition than had previously been observed in telecommunications studies. We believe this phenomenon to be directly linked to communicating with computers. Users seem to demonstrate a need for more exact communication ... Most messages in both modes were simple grammatical constructions or incomplete, simple grammatical constructions. There were, however, in the voice mode some cases of very complex grammatical constructions' (Zoltan et al. 1982:291).

For the two studies with User Specialty Languages in which errors were analyzed, the typing errors were 2.1% (152 of 7278 queries in Grades) and 6.3% (49 of 726 queries in Rooms). There was almost no ungrammatical input (14 of 7278 in Grades). So the many small errors reported by Chapanis (1973) for interpersonal communication by voice do not seem to be a problem for natural language communication with computers.

On the subject of ungrammatical questions, Krause (1982:96-97) gives two examples that are interesting because of their motivation. When the user was asked about his language use, he replied that he had wanted to adapt to the machine. The examples are:

Welche Deutschnote in Quarta hat wieviele Schüler
Which Germangrade in class7 has how many students

Wieviele Schüler repetieren 1 Klassen
How many students repeat 1 classes

In the first case, he assumed that it would be easier for the machine to find the data if the order of nounphrases in the question reflected the way the corresponding data was stored in the relation. When the system did not understand, he tried (successfully) the grammatical version of his question. In the second case, the ungrammatical form led to the correct answer, due to an error in the syntax. Then the user explained in detail why the ungrammatical form was better for the system.

Similar commentaries were given with formal styles like what is the name of for who is, or with overspecified queries like which employees work for manager Smith, and list all employees when who works for Smith, and list (the) employees would have produced the same result.

An assumption we made from the early studies (Lehmann et al. 1978), that people expect different pragmatics with a computer than they do in dialogue with other people, seems to be supported by Krause (1982) and Zoltan et al. (1982). This leads to more careful typing or speaking and fewer errors on the one hand, on the other hand it can lead to grammatical adaptation similar to what Ferguson (1969) observed about talking to foreigners. If the expectations are in fact different, then human factors requirements for computers that are derived from the properties of interpersonal communication (cf. Maas, 1982) are applicable only where people behave in the same way or closely similar ways with computers as they do with other people. According to Zoltan et al. (1982) the measures for problem solution time and word count, e. g., are different for voice and written modes, but the difference is the same in person to computer communication as in person to person communication. Comparison of individual apects of human communication in person to person and person to computer situations can show where features of human communication conform or run counter to what people expect of a computer.

4.5 SEMANTIC OVERSHOOT

Shneiderman (1978) points out that not knowing the data base may play an important role in the number of 'irrelevant' questions that his natural language subjects asked, i. e. questions for which there was not data.

In our studies, there were very few questions that went beyond the data base. Most of them were not questions to the data base, but to the developers, like: How can I get this thing to accept more than

<u>one line</u> (before we eliminated the need for a continuation character). However, such questions did come from visitors to whom we demonstrated the system. The information we gave them: 'this is a small pseudo personnel data base' says what data might be available, but it is not enough to identify all and only the data stored. The reason for this difference in behavior may very well be that the users knew their data, but the visitors did not know ours.

With a formal language, it is already part of the instruction in the language that everything, including field names, must be correctly spelled and that the form of field names, even if they are derived from natural language words, is not predictable from the word itself (DEPARTMENT, DEPT, DEPTNO, ..., see also Jørgensen et al. 1982 and the references there). Therefore: In order to ask for information on Smith's address, one must look for the name of the data field containing addresses. At this point one would find that there is no such field and not put the query. As a result, there is no record of the questions users meant to ask but found that there is no data before querying the system.

It might be interesting to try to elicit questions beyond the data base with a formal language. Maybe using one relation with many fields, where the field names are unabbreviated natural language words. A large number of fields is important so that there is a choice between looking through a long list for presence of a word or putting a query. If the list looks as if the field names are predictable, people might put queries without consulting the list and then also query data that are not available.

4.6 TRAINING

A major argument for natural language communication with computers is that it would eliminate the need for training. It is doubtful whether training can ever be dispensed with, even with more powerful and less restricted systems. With USL, training is still needed. Knowing what views and vocabulary to define and deciding on the shape of views is a major problem. Only syntactic correctness and completeness of a definition can really be taken over by a prompting routine. In principle, view and vocabulary definition is straightforward. Assuming that personnel data is available in the following relation:

PER(EMPLOYEENUMBER,NAME,ADDRESS,BIRTHDATE,MANAGER,FROM,TILL)

the views can be defined as projections of the appropriate columns of PER:

ADDRESS(NOM_ADDRESS,OF_EMPLOYEENUMBER)
MANAGER(NOM_MANAGER,OF_EMPLOYEENUMBER,TS_FROM,TG_TILL)

The difficulties lie e. g. in realizing that, as long as addresses are defined only as addresses of personnel numbers, one can ask for the address of 43567, but not for the address of Smith. If there are many people named Smith in the data base, one will probably not want to do that, but the point is that having to make these decisions and making them must be learned.

Apart from knowing their data and vocabulary, which they either had defined themselves with our help or which we had defined in close contact with them, we definitely needed to train users to:

expect and not worry about ambiguities
expect and recognize restrictions
react to diagnostics

Our system was not designed for casual users and will not work for them now. It would need major extensions for allowing them to 'zoom in' on the data and vocabulary that is available. This is not needed for users who know their data and can define new words when they need them. But they still must learn whether they need a synonym or a new view.

4.7 PERFORMANCE

One argument that has now become obsolete is that of the overhead in time required by natural language front ends. Compared to other systems and most of all compared to search times in a relational data base of more than demonstration size, the added time required for the natural language front end becomes negligible. In User Specialty Languages it takes seconds to analyze the input and generate the code, while it may take several minutes to execute the query. Details on times for parsing and interpretation are found in Grüber (1982).

5 CONCLUSION

We assumed when we started that natural language would be good human factors per se, no adjustments needed. However we found that there were good and bad human factors of the system that had nothing to do with natural language. Formatting hurt much more than lacking constructions. Defining relations and vocabulary, thinking of how one was going to use words, rather than do systems analysis and design the most advanced data base ever, proved difficult, particularly for computer people. One aspect we consider to be very good human factors: Users know their language always much better than the machine, they complain if the system responds in an unexpected way. This is different from any formal language, where users, particularly naive users alswaysfeel slightly insecure and are ready to check several times before they assume a system error.

The results of the studies show that natural language questions do not require more typing than formal language expressions, natural language questions are often shorter. We are often not aware of their complexity because we are so used to this way of expressing ourselves. Restrictions are acceptable, but there are differences in how easily they can be learned. Purely syntactic resctrictions should be avoided. It could not be observed that natural language inputs were often ungrammatical and full of errors. Where ungrammatical input or deviant language behavior occurred, the intention often was to behave in a manner appropriate for communicating with the machine. This supports the assumption that people expect different pragmatics when interacting with a machine and requires caution in transferring observations made in person to person communication.

On the other hand, the users can certainly formulate the questions that would answer their information needs. They are confident about their language use, but prepared to meet the system half-way. So it seems as if even with a system with restricted capabilities, with its instable behavior in the experimental stage, and despite its hardly userfriendly messages, more of the expected advantages of natural language can be observed than of the suggested disadvantages.

6 ACKNOWLEDGEMENT

I wish to acknowledge Dr. Albrecht Blaser for reading and commenting on this paper, Klaus Horländer and Dirk Bethe for counting the quantifiers, and Michael Holz and Dr. Robert Herr for technical support.

7 REFERENCES

Bach, E. (1967): have and be in English syntax. Language 43. 462-485.

Bertrand, O., Daudenarde, J. J., du Castel, B. (1981): User Language Generator: Program description/operation manual. Paris, IBM France.

Chamberlin, D. D., Astrahan, M.M., King, W. F., Lorie, R. A., Mehl, J. W., Price, G. T., Schkolnick, M., Selinger, P. Griffiths, Slutz, D. R., Wade, B. W., Jost, R. A. (1981): Support for repetitive transactions and ad hoc queries. ACM Transactions on Data Base Systems 6. 70-94.

Chang, C. L., (1978): Finding missing joins for incomplete queries in relational data bases. IBM Research Laboratory, San Jose, California, RJ2145.

Chapanis, A. (1973): The communication of factual information through various channels. Information Storage and Retrieval 9:215-231.

Damerau, F. J. (1979): The transformational query answering system (TQA) operational statistics. IBM Research Report RC 7739. Yorktown Heights, New York.

Ferguson, C. A. (1969): Foreigner talk. Proceedings of the Third International Congress of Applied Linguistics. Cambridge.

Gaines, B. R. (1981): The technology of interaction - dialogue programming rules. International Journal of Man-Machine Studies 14:133-150.

Grüber, G. (1982): Parsingzeiten in einem natürlichsprachlichen Frage-Antwort-System. Heidelberg Scientific Center TN 82.03.

Habel, Ch., Schmidt, A., Schweppe, H. (1977): BEAST - Ein Übersetzungssystem zur natürlichsprachlichen Kommunikation mit Datenbasen. Semantic Network Project Report 4, Informatik, TU Berlin.

Henisz-Thompson, B. (1978): REL English for the user. California Institute of Technology, Pasadena, California.

Hill, I. D. (1972): Wouldn't it be nice if we could write computer programs in ordinary English - or would it? The Computer Bulletin 306-312.

Jørgensen, A. H., Barnard, P., Hammond, N., Clark, I. (1982): Naming commands: An analysis of designers' naming behavior. Paper presented at Cognitive Engineering: A conference on the psychology of problem solving with computers, Vrije Universiteit Amsterdam, 10-13 Augustus 1982.

Kay, M. (1967): Experiments with a powerful parser. Second International Conference on Computational Linguistics, Grenoble, August 1967.

Kelly, M. J. and Chapanis, A. (1977): Limited vocabulary natural language dialogue. International Journal of Man-Machine Studies, 9:479-501.

Kettler, W., Schmidt, A., Zoeppritz, M. (1981): Erfahrungen mit zwei natürlich-sprachlichen Abfragesystemen. Heidelberg Scientific Center TR 81.01.001.

Krause, J. (1979): Preliminary results of a user study with the 'User Specialty Languages' System and consequences for the architecture of natural language interfaces. Heidelberg Scientific Center, TR 79.04.003.

Krause, J. (1980a): Natural language access to information systems: An evaluation study of its acceptance by endusers. Information Systems 5:297-318.

Krause, J. (1980b): Mensch-Maschine-Interaktion in natürlicher Sprache: Zur Bewertung eines natürlichsprachigen Frage-Antwort-Systems. R. Kuhlen (ed.): Datenbasen, Datenbanken, Netzwerke: Praxis des Information Retrieval. Vol. 3: Nutzung und Bewertung von Retrievalsystemen. München: K.G. Saur, 199-229.

Krause, J. (1982): Mensch-Maschine-Interaktion in natürlicher Sprache. Tübingen: Niemeyer.

Lehmann, H., Ott, N., Zoeppritz, M. (1977): Language facilities of USL/German, Version III. IBM Germany Heidelberg Scientific Center, TN 77.04.

Lehmann, H. (1978a): 'Interpretation of natural language in an information system' IBM Journal of research and development 22:560-572. Previously TR 77.11.006.

Lehmann H. (1978b): The USL Project - Its objectives and status, Relational data base systems, Proceedings of the International Technical Conference held at the IBM Scientific Center, Bari, Italy.

Lehmann, H., Ott, N., Zoeppritz, M. (1978): User experiments with natural language for data base access. Proceedings of the 7th International Conference on Computational Linguistics, Bergen 14th to 18th August 1978. Short version in German: Zoeppritz (1978): Erste Erfahrungen mit der Benutzung des USL-Systems. S. Schindler, W. K. Giloi (eds.): Proceedings of the 8th Annual Meeting of the Gesellschaft für Informatik (GI), October 2 - 3, 1979, . short papers.

Lehmann, H. (1979): The USL System for data analysis. Proceedings of the Workshop on Natural Language for Interaction with Data Bases, IIASA, Laxenburg, Austria.

Lehmann, H. Krause, J. (1979): User Specialty Languages: A natural language base information system and its evaluation. Proceedings

of the joint annual meeting of LDV-Fittings and the Association of
Literary and Linguistic Computing, Bonn, December 12 - 14, 1979.

Lehmann, H., Blaser, A. (1979): Query languages in data base systems
TR 79.07.004 IBM Heidelberg Scientific Center. Short version in
K. H. Böhling, P. P. Spies (eds.): Proceedings of the 9th Annual
Meeting of the Gesellschaft für Informatik (GI). Berlin: Springer
64-80.

Lehmann, H. (1980): A system for answering questions in German.
Proceedings 6th International ALLC Symposium, Cambridge, England,
March 28 - April 3, 1980.

Lehmann, H., Ott, N. (forthcoming): Interpretation routines of the
User Specialty Languages System.

Maas, S. (1982): Why systems transparency. Proceedings Cognitive
Engineering: A conference on the psychology of problem solving
with computers, Vrije Universiteit Amsterdam, 10-13 Augustus 1982,
177-184.

Michaelis, P. R., Chapanis, A., Weeks, G. D. Kelly, M. (1977): Word
usage in interactive dialog with restricted and unrestricted
vocabularies. IEEE Transactions on Professional Communication,
PC-20(4):214-221.

Montgomery, C. A. (1972): Is natural language an unnatural query
language? Proceedings of the ACM National Conference 1075-1078.
ACM New York.

Ott, N., Zoeppritz, M. (1979): USL - An experimental information
system based on natural language L. Bolc (ed.): Natural language
based computer systems. Natural communication with computers, vol.
2.256-282. München, Wien: Carl Hanser-Verlag, London, Melbourne:
Macmillan.

Ott, N. (1979a): Bericht über die KFG-Studie. Heidelberg Scientific
Center TN 79.03.

Ott, N. (1979a): Das experimentelle, auf natürlicher Sprache
basierende Informationssystem USL, Nachrichten für Dokumentation
30:129-139.

Ott, N., Horländer, K. (1982): Removing redundant join operations
involving views. IBM Germany Heidelberg Scientific Center, TR
82.03.003.

Pirotte, A. (1978): Linguistic aspects of high-level relational
languages. Report R367, MBLE Research Laboratory, Brussels.

Purnadi, H., A. (1981): Vergleich einer natürlichen Abfragesprache
(USL) mit der formalen Abfragesprache einer gegebenen Datenbank
(IQRP). Diploma thesis, Fachhochschule Ravensburg.

Reisner, P. (1977): Use of psychological experimentation as an aid to
development of a query language. IEEE Transactions on Software
Engineering, SE-3:218-229.

Sammet, J. E. (1969): Programming languages: history and
fundamentals. Prentice Hall International.

Shneiderman, B. (1978): Improving the human factors aspect of data base interaction. ACM Transactions on Database Systems 3:417-439.

Shneiderman, B. (1981): A note on human factors issues of natural language interaction with database systems. Information Systems 6:126-129.

Tennant, H. (1979): Experience with the evaluation of natural language question answerers. Working Paper 18, Advanced Automation Group, Coordinated Science Laboratory, University of Illinois at Urbana-Champaign, Urbana, Ill.

Thomas, J. C., Gould, John, D. (1975): A psychological study of Query By Example. AFIPS Conference Proceedings, 1975 National Computer Conference, vol. 44:439-445.

Thomas, J. C. (1976): Quantifiers and question-asking. IBM Research Report RC 5866.

Thompson, F. B., Lockemann, P. C., Dostert, B. H., Deverill, R. S. (1969): REL: A rapidly extensible language system. Proceedings 24th National ACM Conference, New York, August 1969.

Todd, S. J. P., (1975): PRTV - A technical overview. IBM Scientific Center Peterlee, England, TR UKSC 0075. Also in IBM Systems Journal 15. 285-308, 1976.

Turner, J., Jarke, M., Stohr, E., Vassiliou, Y., White, N. (1982): Using restricted natural language for data retrieval - a field evaluation. Proceedings NYU Symposium on User Interfaces, May 26-28, 1982.

Woods, W. A., Kaplan, R. J., Nash-Webber, B. (1972): The Lunar Sciences Natural Language Information System: Final Report. BBN Report 2378, Bolt, Beranek and Newman, Inc., Cambridge, Mass.

Woods, W. A. (1977): A personal view of natural language understanding. SIGART Newsletters 61:17-20.

Zloof, M. (1974): Query By Example. IBM Technical Report RC 4971.

Zoeppritz, M. (1979): A note on WIEVIEL - HOW MANY. IBM Germany Heidelberg Scientific Center, TN 79.02.

Zoeppritz, M. (manuscript): Syntax for German in the User Specialty Languages System.

Zoltan, E., Weeks, G. D., Ford, W. R. (1982): Natural language communication with computers: A comparison of voice and keyboard input. In G. Johannsen, J. E. Rijsdorp (eds.): Analysis, Design, and Evaluation of Man-Machine Systems, IFAC/IFIP/IFORS/IEA Conference, Baden-Baden, Federal Republic of Germany, September 27-28, 1982.

ANALYTIC TOOLS FOR HUMAN FACTORS OF SOFTWARE

Phyllis Reisner
IBM Research Laboratory
San Jose, CA

ABSTRACT: Behavioral experiments are currently the primary method of assessing the human factors of end user systems. Such experiments, however, are time consuming and sometimes come too late in the development cycle to influence ease of use. Analytic tools, which involve an abstract representation of a user interface and some manipulation of that representation to predict ease of use, are potentially faster. They can also be more intellectually satisfying. This paper gives examples of some analytic tools currently being developed and discusses the motivation and state of the art of such tools.

INTRODUCTION

Most human factors studies of end user systems are behavioral experiments. This is as it should be. Real use is the most direct way to find out whether a system is easy to use. However, behavioral tests are costly and time consuming. They can come so late in the cycle of developing an end user system that the results are ignored. Fortunately, though, science and technology develop along more than one path. One is empirical (try it out) and the other is analytic (study its components abstractly). Analytical studies may be a less costly and faster way to study the human factors of end user systems.

Primarily in academia and in industrial research laboratories, some researchers have begun to develop analytic tools to determine the ease of use of software. This paper gives examples of some of these studies. This is not yet a clearly developed trend. It is more a trickle than a trend. However, the direction is sufficiently important to merit attention.

The word "tool" in the "analytic tools" to be discussed in this paper is being used in a very broad sense. The analytic tools to be discussed are methods of determining the ease of use of a system.

The studies to be discussed thus fall in the realm of methodology development, rather than studies of particular systems, or studies of principles of human factors. A simple analogy should make this concrete. Behavioral tests of end user systems measure ease of use very much as a ruler measures the height of a table. These studies are not concerned with measuring tables; they are developing rulers.

To put this trend in perspective, the paper first gives some general background about human factors goals and about the behavioral experiments that are commonly used to attain these goals. Then it describes some problems in the behavioral approach that cause researchers to look for analytic methods that might avoid these problems. The background section also describes what we mean by an analytic tool. The paper then gives examples of some analytic tools currently being developed to attain the same goals as the behavioral ones. Finally, it gives the author's very personal assessment of this trend.

The paper is not an attempt to exhaustively survey work in this area. Rather, it gives examples of the kinds of work currently being performed. The purpose is to show that, although behavioral science dominates human factors, and rightly so, there are some faint glimmers of an analytic approach on the horizon.

BACKGROUND

This background section discusses: some goals of human factors, some steps required for behavioral experiments to achieve these goals, and some problems inherent in such experimentation. It then describes what we mean by an "analytic tool" to achieve these same goals.

GOALS OF HUMAN FACTORS

Human factors studies of end user systems can have a number of different goals. The goals described below can apply to any human factors studies. Consequently, they also apply to human factors of end user systems. Unfortunately, there are too few attempts to apply human factors to end user systems to accomplish these goals.

Some goals are:

o <u>Quality control:</u> These studies measure the ease of use of some particular end user system. The intent of such measurement is to determine whether the system meets previously specified criteria of user performance.

o <u>Purchasing/marketing:</u> Instead of measuring the ease of use of one particular system, these studies compare the ease of use of two or more systems. Such comparison would be useful to a potential buyer of a system. Since comparative ease of use is of concern to the purchaser, it is also of concern to the salesman or to the market analyst who wishes to sell a particular system.

o <u>Designing systems:</u> Human factors studies are used to assist in system design. They do so by providing feedback about user problems. They also permit the designer to determine which of two or more designs is easier to use. In my opinion, this is currently the most important goal.

o <u>Research:</u> A major goal of human factors is to augment our fundamental understanding of ease of use. This goal is primarily of interest to the researcher, who is looking for general design principles applicable to a variety of different systems.

The primary method of attaining these goals is currently to run behavioral experiments with users. We will discuss these next.

<u>BEHAVIORAL TESTS</u>

To make behavioral experimentation concrete, the next section describes some of the steps required to run such experiments. For actual examples of such experiments, the reader should see the book by Shneiderman [1980] and the special issue of the <u>ACM Computing Surveys</u> on "the Psychology of Human-Computer Interaction" [1981]. This section then discusses some problems that the experimental approach creates for the human factors of end user systems.

Steps in Behavioral Experiments

The following steps apply primarily to studies aimed at the first three goals mentioned above, quality control, purchasing/marketing, and system design. Analogous ones apply to the fourth goal, research.

Some of the steps required to run behavioral experiments in this field of end user human factors are:

Obtain a running system: The system to be tested must be available. Usually, but not always, there must be an implemented system on which to run the experiments. This is an extremely serious requirement. If experiments can not be run until a system is ready to be sold to customers, it is too late to influence the design. (For some kinds of tests it is possible to run paper and pencil experiments, cf. Reisner, [1981b]).

Determine the purpose or hypotheses: Once the needed system is available, the purpose of the experiment must be very clearly decided and stated. This seems obvious. However, surprisingly, it is sometimes not done. Determining a reasonable goal can be a more difficult task than one might imagine.

Determine the approach: Once the objective of the experiment is established, a method of approaching the problem must be developed. The general approach to behavioral measurement is to give experimental subjects (people) some tasks (e.g. type a letter) to perform, then to give them a test to measure how well they perform that task (e.g. time to type the letter). However, deciding exactly what kind of tasks and what kinds of tests are appropriate can require inventiveness, common sense, and time. The tasks must be intuitively sensible. The tests must be practical for the given time constraints. Particularly when dealing with systems of non-trivial size, practicality becomes an issue.

Design the experiment: Once the approach has been formulated, the experiment must be designed. Factors other than the ones of interest can influence experimental results. For example, in a comparison of two systems, care must be taken that the people using each system are of roughly equal intelligence. Such factors must be "controlled" experimentally or handled in the later statistical analysis.

The discipline known as "Design of Experiments" is a well-known part of experimental psychology which deals with this problem. This discipline has many ways of "arranging" an experiment to control for such unwanted factors and to select a statistical treatment which is appropriate to the arrangement. However, selection and prioritizing of the factors to be controlled can require considerable intuition and soul-searching - and again, time.

Develop test materials: Once an experiment has been designed, actual preparation of the "test materials" can start. The materials will be used by the experimental subjects in the tasks that will be set for them. Preparation of appropriate test materials can be a very laborious task. However, it must at the same time be done with care and judgement. The materials must be sufficiently comprehensive to justify later claims that one wants to make on the basis of the experimental data. Furthermore, the materials are another source of possible error which the experiment designer must control. For example, statements in English (or other languages) can be ambiguous. If an ambiguous statement is used as part of the test materials, some subjects will interpret it one way, some another. The experimenter will then be unable to make sense of the results.

Obtain experimental subjects: Next, the kind of "experimental subjects" (the people who will be used in the experiment) must be decided upon and a mechanism for obtaining them established. Temporary office workers and college students are usually relatively easy to obtain - but people with - or without - specific skills or abilities can be difficult to obtain. Furthermore, there will be a myriad of details here to be considered. For example, the experimenter has to remember to specify that no color-blind subjects are to be selected if a color display terminal is being tested.

Acquire teaching materials: Ideally, whatever method will be used to teach users the system (unless it is intended to be completely self-explanatory) will be ready and available to the experimenter. In practice, this is frequently not the case. Then the experimenter has to take steps to obtain teaching materials. In the worst case the experimenter prepares the teaching materials him/herself. This should <u>not</u> be done. The experimenter has now become part of the development team and may lack objectivity. But it is sometimes unavoidable. It is also time consuming.

<u>Acquire documentation:</u> Ideally, whatever documentation the user is expected to have available to him will be ready. In practice, this is frequently not the case. The experimenter must then, as in the case of teaching, somehow obtain it.

<u>Develop measurement tools:</u> Measurement tools may have to be developed to obtain the measurements desired. In the case of on-line testing where timing data is required, for example, some mechanism for capturing the data may have to be developed. This might require obtaining special hardware or software - or even of specifying and building it oneself. Even pencil and paper experiments can require development of specific tools or methods. For example, if "number of errors" is to be measured in testing a data base query language, decisions have to be made about what is - and what is not - an error. In some cases it is further necessary to develop a system of classifying errors. Ideally, the classification method should then be tested to see if different people, using it, will get the same results. (Since development of a classification scheme may depend on experimental results, this step may be deferred until after the experiment is run). Again, time is required.

<u>"Debug" the experiment:</u> With everything prepared, it is necessary to run a "pilot" experiment. This is the equivalent of debugging a program. Flaws in conception, in details of subjects, test materials or any components of the experiment have to be found and corrected.

<u>Run the experiment:</u> Finally the experiment can be run. And then more time consuming problems can arise. The better the preparatory steps, of course, the less likely this is to happen. But it still does. Running experiments with people can be unpredictable. Running experiments with computer systems which "crash" can be time-consuming because results of the particular person using the system at the time may have to be discarded and another experimental subject obtained.

<u>Analyze the data:</u> Then the data must be analyzed. This can be quite laborious. It is frequently time consuming.

<u>Perform statistical tests:</u> Finally, of course, whatever statistical analysis is required can be performed.

It is probably clear that good experimentation is not an easy task. It frequently requires both a considerable amount of inventiveness and of drudgery, plus a large admixture of common sense.   A major requirement is <u>time.</u>

In practice not all the steps mentioned above are required for every experiment. In some cases, there simply isn't time. One does the best one can with the time and resources available.   The good experimentalist develops an approach that will be consistent with the time and resources available.   Running a good experiment, just as developing a good system, takes planning, design and development, testing (of the experiment) and actual execution. Throughout, it requires meticulous attention   to detail. It also   requires a considerable amount of what is commonly known as "dog work". The good experimentalist probably requires the same personal skills as the good system designer.

The fact that experimentation is time consuming creates problems for incorporating human factors into end user systems. We turn next to these problems.

<u>PROBLEMS WITH EXPERIMENTATION</u>

Although not every time-consuming step above is required in every experiment, these experiments have one thing in common. They usually are difficult, costly and time consuming to run. This problem has serious consequences.

Because such experiments are costly and time consuming, they are very frequently not run at all. This is unfortunate, particularly in the system design area, where failure to find usability problems during design can be disastrous to the end user. It may also be costly in the market place.   It certainly does nothing to improve the quality of life for people who must use a system which is badly designed from the point of view of the end user.

Another result of the cost and time problem is that experiments are run, but not run well. Too few experimental subjects might be used, for example. Or only initial use of a system is tested, and not long term use.

A further difficulty is that an implemented system is usually required on which to perform the experiments. At very least, a simulation or prototype is frequently needed. By the time such a system is available, it may be too late for experiments to actually aid in system design.

One last difficulty with experimentation is important. Experiments of the first three kinds mentioned above do not embody theoretical understanding of principles of human factors. This is intellectually unsatisfying. The experiments tell us whether a system meets its usability goals, or which of two systems is easier to use, or where users make mistakes. They do not tell us why these results are obtained. Analytic tools, on the other hand, have embedded in them the reasons that such results will happen.

For the reasons above, analytic tools such as the ones we now describe are required. The next section describes what we mean by an "analytic tool".

ANALYTIC TOOLS: DESCRIPTION AND REQUIREMENTS

Given the fact that experiments are slow and costly, analytic tools are desirable. What then, is an "analytic tool" for human factors? Just as the term "tool" was used in a very broad sense, the term "analytic tool" is also being used very broadly. In an analytic tool there is:

    o some abstract representation of relevant aspects of the end user interface, and

    o some examination or manipulation of that representation in order to predict what would happen if actual users were to use the system.

The abstract representation in the first statement is a _model_ of the reality to be examined. It makes a statement about which particular aspects of a system are related to ease of use. It also provides a representation of those aspects.

The key concept in the last statement above is <u>prediction.</u> An analytic tool does not measure ease of use directly by actually measuring human behavior.   It predicts what would happen <u>if ease of use were measured.</u>

There are two practical requirements for analytic tools in this area. First, once a tool has been developed, it must be validated. That is, we need to know whether the tool does indeed make correct predictions about ease of use. The general method of validating such a tool is to run behavioral experiments. However, these are experiments to test the tool. They are not experiments to test a particular system for ease of use.

The second practical requirement for a tool to predict ease of use is that the tool itself be easy to use. To find out whether this is so, again, behavioral studies are needed. However, these studies measure the human factors of the tool, not of the system that the tool measures.

These four points define and describe an analytic tool.

SOME ANALYTIC TOOLS

This section describes some analytic tools that have been or are being developed. The first two papers discuss keystroke-type approaches. Central to these approaches are counts of the number of keystrokes required to perform some task. The next section discusses what we call "language" approaches. Although the approaches use different kinds of models, some notion of language, or of language-like structure, is embodied in each.

The studies to be discussed have a number of different purposes or goals. Most are attempts to aid system design, but there are also examples of the other goals described in the background section. For each approach we will discuss the following:

    o the purpose
    o the model

o the analysis method used to predict ease of use from the
  model,
  and

o the validation studies

Since none of the tools have been tested for ease of use, we will
omit discussion of this factor.

KEYSTROKE-TYPE APPROACHES

The two papers which follow both attempt to predict the time it will
take users to perform various tasks in interactive systems. Central
to both of them is a simple count of the number of keystrokes
necessary to perform a task, hence the term "keystroke-type" models.
However, there is a subtle, but very important, difference between
them.

The Embley et. al. Keystroke Approach

Purpose: The purpose of the model proposed by Embley, Lan, Leinbaugh
and Nagy [Embley, 1978] is to compare program editors "from the point
of view of the end user". The basis for the comparison is the time
it would take to perform a set of tasks using the relevant editor.
Quite reasonably, the editor which takes less time to perform a set
of tasks can be claimed to be easier to use. By way of example,
Embley et. al. use their approach to compare two different editors
available at the University of Nebraska. The particular editors
(NUROS and CMS) are described in their paper. The work is thus a
comparative system analysis. From the .example in the paper, this
work appears to fit primarily into the second goal in the framework
above, "purchasing/marketing". With no desire to slight his
colleagues, I will refer to this work as "the Embley model", for
brevity.

Model: In the Embley model, total time to perform some "unit" task
consists of two main factors: the time to key-in the commands and
another factor. The second factor consists of mental preparation, or
"think" time, and computer response time. The mental preparation time
is the time for the user to decide what to do next. Time to key-in
commands is taken as the number of keystrokes times the average time
per keystroke.

The time for a task is thus just:

$$T_{task} = mT_c + nT_k$$

where

m is the number of command-response pairs
n is the number of
  keystrokes.
c is the time per command for mental preparation
  and for computer response
k is the time per keystroke

Analysis: The analysis procedure is simply to count the number of
keystrokes and the number of commands, and to apply the formula. The
data can be captured by the computer. Some estimate of the parameters
for think-response time and for time per keystroke is also required.

Validation: The model has not been empirically validated. This
would require:

  o independent estimates of the parameters
  o application of the model
  o prediction of task times
  o experiments to determine task times empirically, and
  o comparison of predicted and empirically determined times.

However, the authors did apply the formula to several program editing
tasks using the NUROS and CMS editors. Using parameters of T_c = 5
seconds and T_k = 1/2 second, they found statistically significant
differences between the two editors.

The Card and Moran Keystroke-level Approach

Card and Moran [Card, 1980] also have a model based on keystrokes.
They call it the keystroke-level model, emphasizing the word "level".
Operations other than keystrokes are included in the model, but these
are of about the same "time grain" as keystrokes - hence the term
"keystroke level".

Purpose: The keystroke level model is viewed very explicitly by Card and Moran as a system design tool. It is intended to be used during the design of an interactive system. The model is intended to predict task time, for expert users, on routine tasks. The precise method (sequence of commands) must be specified, and the performance is not expected to contain errors.

Model: Like the Embley model, the keystroke-level model counts keystrokes. However, there are a number of other parameters included. There are four physical-motor parameters: Keystroking, Pointing (as with a mouse), Homing (moving the hands to the appropriate physical device, and Drawing (drawing straight line segments, using the mouse). In addition, there is a parameter for Mental Preparation (e.g. deciding which command to call). There is also a parameter for system response time. Time to execute a task is the sum of the times for the relevant parameters. Unlike the Embley model, which is a data driven model, the keystroke model is very clearly and very explicitly a model of the user.

Analysis: Card and Moran present detailed rules for applying their formula. Of particular importance are the rules for when to place an M (mental operator) in the equation. These are based on assumptions about "chunking", a concept well-known in cognitive psychology which states that people process information in chunks, or large conceptual units. In psychology, the size of a chunk varies with expertise and experience. The analysis method is then simply the application of the formula.

Validation: Card and Moran did run a large number of careful validation experiments (28 users, 10 systems, 14 tasks). They predicted times for the tasks from their formula, correctly obtaining times for each parameter (except Mental Preparation) from sources outside the experiment. Only error-free data was used. They then compared the predictions to the experimental results and found that the model predicted task times with reasonable accuracy (rms error 21 percent of average predicted execution time). They feel that "any new proposal (for a model) must do better than the Keystroke-Level Model... to merit serious consideration."

LANGUAGE-TYPE APPROACHES

The next group of approaches to be discussed all involve "language-type" models. They model man-machine interaction with tools that have traditionally been used to describe either natural or computer languages. Central to all these representation techniques is the notion of structure. A language (and hence the modelled part of an interaction) is viewed as more than just a sequence of "words". There are assumed to be classes of words. Only certain sequences of such classes become acceptable sequences, or "sentences" in the language.

The first two papers use a BNF-like grammar to aid in system design. The next paper also uses BNF, but for research into system design. The last paper provides a comprehensive framework for describing user interfaces. It only consists of models, and only suggests analysis metrics briefly, without examples. However, it is included here because it may be very influential.

The Reisner Action Language Model (ROBART)

The work being done at IBM San Jose attempts to model the actions of the user at a terminal with a formal grammar. There are two related efforts in this direction. In the first, two versions of a small color graphics system (ROBART) were described with a formal grammar, predictions about ease of use were made, and exploratory tests were run to determine whether the predictions were correct. There were a number of areas in this endeavor which required further work. The second effort uses a text editor (SPF) instead of the color graphics system for its example.

This section describes the ROBART approach [Reisner, 1981a].

Purpose: The work to develop an Action Language Grammar is an attempt to provide a system design tool. The intent is to provide a predictive tool which will accomplish two goals:

- o compare alternative designs
  for ease of use, and
- o identify design choices which could cause
  users to make mistakes.

The ROBART systems: The function of both color graphics systems was the same. With either system, it was possible to draw colored lines, circles or rectangles, type text in color, or draw "continuous" (etch-a-sketch like) shapes by sweeping a cursor about the screen. Cursor movement was controlled by a joystick. However, the user interface for the two systems differed. Since the function was the same in both systems (e.g. draw a colored circle) but the interfaces differed, this was an excellent experimental situation. Differences in function were "controlled". Thus, experimental differences between the two systems were more likely to be attributable to differences between the interfaces than if this were not so. Briefly, the following differences are crucial to the later validation.

1. There were differences in the number of steps required to "select" different shapes within ROBART 1 (e.g. more steps for circle than for line).

2. The number of steps to select corresponding shapes in ROBART 2 was less than in ROBART 1. (e.g. drawing a circle in ROBART 2 required fewer steps than in ROBART 1).

3. Within ROBART 1, there were two methods for "initiating" a shape (giving the first parameter for location on the screen, etc). IN ROBART 2, there was only one method.

These differences and problems were identifiable in the formal description.

Model: The Action Language Model views user actions at an input terminal (keying, moving a joystick, pressing a button) as a language. It describes that language with a notation which is well-known to both linguists and to computer scientists. The notation is variously known as BNF, Backus-Naur Form, or production-rule notation. It describes a language with a set of rules, or productions. Any particular sentence can then be described by the particular rules for producing it. A tree structure is often used to illustrate the structure of particular sentences. Figure 1 shows a small set of rules for a sentence in English. Terminal symbols (words) are represented in capital letters, "parts of speech" (e.g. noun phrase, verb phrase) in small ones.

```
Example: "The chairs  are too hard"
         |_____||_____|
              np            vp



Rules:


            S -> noun phrase + verb phrase
 noun phrase -> article + noun
     article -> THE
        noun -> CHAIRS
 verb phrase -> verb + noun phrase
                    .
                    .
                    .
```

Figure 1.   Some Production Rules for a Sentence in English

A few rules for a ROBART grammar are given in Figure 2.   The symbol
"|" means "or". The symbol "+" means "followed by".   The rules are
somewhat abbreviated. To maintain the "action language" concept, they
should be read as actions. For example, the first rule is "to create
a picture, create a colored shape or a series of colored shapes".
Description of the ROBART system and details on how to read the
notation are given in [Reisner, 1981a].

```
picture -> colored shape | picture + colored shape
colored shape -> color + shape | shape + color
color -> CURSOR IN RED | CURSOR IN BLUE | ...
shape -> ......
```

Figure 2. A few rules in a ROBART grammar

<u>Analysis:</u> Two criteria were used to analyse designs in these grammars:

    o the length of sentences to be compared
    o the number of "extra" rules in the grammar

The latter was taken as an indicator of inconsistency in the language. This requires explanation. In English, there are two ways of creating a past tense. For the weak verbs, the ending "-ed" is added to the stem. (e.g. walk -> walked). For the strong verbs, there is a change in the stem (e.g. go -> went). There are thus two ways to create a past tense in English, represented by two rules. The existence of two rules, where a person could reasonably expect one, creates problems for the new user of English. Thus many children will spontaneously say, "yesterday I goed to the store", using the wrong generalization about how to make a past tense in English. From the point of view of the new user, English is inconsistent. This inconsistency causes him/her to make mistakes. This fact is embodied in the existence of two rules where one would suffice.

In addition to the two criteria actually used to analyze ease of use in this work, other possibilities were noted but not explored: the number of different terminal symbols (words), the number of alternations in hand or eye position, the total number of rules needed to describe some subset of the language, and other measures of sentence complexity used by linguists.

<u>Validation:</u> The predictions made from the action language model were validated, but only by some preliminary experiments. The method was to compare predictions from the model with behavioral experiments. Specifically, based on the lengths of the strings, predictions were made that:

    o selecting shapes in ROBART 1 would vary in difficulty
    o selecting shapes in ROBART 2 would not vary in difficulty
    o selecting shapes in ROBART 1 would be harder than in ROBART 2.

Results of behavioral tests are shown in Figure 3. They supported the predictions.

	ROBART 1	ROBART 2
line	0	0
box	4	1
circle	8	0
continuous line	2	0
continuous box	6	0
continuous circle	9	1

Figure 3. Number of subjects (of 10) unable
to select the given shape

There was another prediction tested. This prediction was based on the
criterion of "extra rules". Specifically, there were two rules in
ROBART 1 where ROBART 2 had only one. This represented an
inconsistency in ROBART 1. The method for initiating one particular
kind of shape (a "discrete" shape) in ROBART 1 involved setting some
switches and pressing some buttons. To select another kind of shape
(a "continuous" shape) involved turning a knob on a joystick. From
the fact that there was an extra rule, a prediction was that users
would use the wrong method for selecting shapes. In fact, 70% of the
users made the expected error. In ROBART 2, on the other hand, there
was only one method; no error was expected, and none observed. Thus,
a very specific error was anticipated, and was found by behavioral
tests. However, there were flaws in the methodology and in the test
procedure. These prompted further development of the methodology and
a more rigorous testing procedure.

The Reisner Action Language Approach (SPF)

Purpose: There were a number of areas in the ROBART work described
above which required further development. Therefore it was decided
to further develop the approach, this time in the context of an IBM
text editor, the SPF editor. In the new approach Reisner, [in
press], shows that "cognition" can be included explicitly in the
grammar and specifies an explicit prediction method. Currently, very
carefully controlled validation experiments are being run.

Model: The grammar in the SPF work consists of two kinds of symbols: physical action symbols and "cognitive" symbols. The physical action symbols represent actions such as pressing a key, turning a knob, pointing with a light pen, etc. These are observable physical actions that serve as input to the system. The cognitive symbols represent cognitive actions, mental behaviors such as performing mental calculation, or remembering the syntax for a command. An example of a portion of a grammar including cognitive actions is shown in Figure 4. Dn is a function in the editor which deletes n lines of text. Cognitive symbols are enclosed in brackets.

```
employ Dn                        ->  <retrieve info. on Dn syntax>
                                     + use Dn
<retrieve info. on Dn syntax>    ->  <retrieve from human memory>
                                     |<retrieve from external source>
<retrieve from human memory>     ->  <RETRIEVE FROM LONG TERM MEMORY>
                                     | <RETRIEVE FROM WORKING MEMORY>
                                     | <USE MUSCLE MEMORY>
retrieve from external source    ->  RETRIEVE FROM BOOK | ASK  SOMEONE
                                     | EXPERIMENT | USE ON-LINE HELP
use Dn                           ->  identify first line
                                     + enter Dn command
                                     + PRESS ENTER
identify first line              ->  ...
enter Dn command                 ->  TYPE D + type n
   ...
```

Figure 4. Part of a grammar for a delete command in a text editor, showing cognitive actions.

Analysis: An explicit analysis process is now used. The process includes the notion of "prediction assumptions" - assumptions about human abilities that are known or obtainable by behavioral measurement. The assumptions are expressed as mathematical inequalities. An example is that the time to perform some specific mental computation is greater than the time for some number of keypresses. The method is:

1. Describe the action language with a formal grammar. Include cognitive actions in the description.
2. Derive sentences from the grammar for the functions to be compared.
3. Convert the sentences to equations with time or errors as the variables.
4. State the prediction assumptions explicitly.
5. Substitute the prediction assumptions in the equations and solve the resulting equations with simple algebra.

The method thus starts with a grammatical description, but ends with simple computation of the parameters that behavioral tests will measure (time or errors).

Validation: Validation of the SPF approach is in progress. It is intended to overcome a possible bias in the preliminary experiments with ROBART. In the ROBART experiments, the same person designed the ROBART 2 interface, wrote the grammars and ran the experiments. Such a situation is not free from the possibility of bias. For experimenting with the SPF editor, therefore, one person is making predictions and another person, (Dr. A. B. Farrand), working independently, is designing and running validation experiments. The predictions and experiments concern relative difficulty of specific functions with the editor, such as Dn (delete n lines, starting with a marked line), and DD (delete a block of lines between the marked first and last ones). So far, predictions and results agree.

The Dunsmore Approach: Using Action Language Grammars for Research

Purpose: Action language grammars are being used by Dunsmore [1982a, 1982b] to compare specific alternative design issues. The issues are general in that results can apply to many different user interfaces. This endeavor thus falls under the fourth, "research", goal above. The context of Dunsmores's work is an attempt to design an interactive system for non-programmer users.

Model and Analysis: Dunsmore uses a BNF representation of user actions as his model. The analysis is based on the number of terminal symbols, on the lengths of the strings, and on the number of rules in a derivation of the strings.

<u>Validation:</u>   Dunsmore makes predictions about alternative designs
from the formal grammar representation, then runs behavioral tests to
determine whether the predictions are correct. Examples of his
predictions and results are:

   o Subjects would be more productive (answer more test questions
   using an information retrieval type on-line system) with a
   small amount of documentation in printed form rather than with
   on-line documentation.   (Result: subjects were nearly twice as
   productive with the printed documentation).

   o Subjects would be slightly more productive with a version of
   the system with "uncrowded"   display formatting (items on
   separate lines) than with a "crowded" display (fewer lines, to
   save space). (Result: Subjects were about 20% more productive
   with the uncrowded version).

The Moran Command Language Grammar

Moran [1981] has presented a comprehensive framework for describing
user interfaces. The method is intended to describe both the user's
"conceptual model" of the system and be useful during the design
process. He calls it a "grammar" because "it can be used to generate
a wide variety of command language system descriptions". The grammar
is too complex to do justice to in a brief overview. Some of its
components will be described briefly.   Interested readers should
refer to the original document.

<u>Purpose:</u> Moran sees CLG as "a tool for helping the designer generate
and evaluate alternative designs for a system". Moran emphasizes
that it is a design representation, not a design methodology. It
falls in the third, system design, category of goals. Moran also sees
CLG as "an analysis of the structure of command language systems",
and as a "model of the different kinds of knowledge that users have
about a system".

<u>Formalism:</u> CLG describes a system from the most abstract,
"conceptual" level to the most detailed embodiment in a physical
device. Moran defines three main components of CLG. Each component
consists of several levels, and there are predefined primitives
within each component. The components are intended to "map' onto

each other: first the conceptual model, then the command language, then the physical embodiment in hardware.

There are three main components of the CLG:

- o Conceptual Component
- o Communication Component
- o Physical Component

The conceptual component contains the abstract concepts central to the user interface; the communication component contains the command language and interactive dialog; and the physical component contains the physical devices that the user comes in contact with.

Each component consists of several "levels". The conceptual component consists of a "task" level (the set of tasks the user wants to accomplish) and a "semantic level" (the concepts and manipulations of objects in the system). The communication component consists of a "syntactic level" (e.g. the command language structure) and an interaction level (consisting of "a fixed set of parts from which all user-system interactions can be described", physical input devices, and other elements).

Within the various levels, Moran specifies a set of entities, tasks, procedures, and methods appropriate to that level. For example, some prespecified entities at the interaction level are: PROMPT, BODY, TERMINATION, RESPONSE, INTERPRETATION.

Several different kinds of notations are used for different components of CLG. The notational system is primarily a structured kind of English notation. The predefined entities act as placeholders which are filled-in with English language statements. There are also programming like constructs (FOR, DO .... UNTIL, REPEAT). The reader is referred to the original article for examples.

Analysis: CLG is presented as an organizing framework for interface designs. Analysis methods for predicting ease of use have not yet been specified. However, Moran does envisage the possibility of deriving a number of different evaluation measures from the description. Among them are efficiency (speed), from a weighted sum of the primitive actions - as in the keystroke model. Other suggestions are that it should be possible to compute memory load, learning time, etc, from the various components. Examples of applying these suggestions are not given.

Validation: Since the suggested evaluation measures (other than the keystroke model) have not yet been specified in detail or examples in running systems given, it is premature to speak of validation.

DISCUSSION

This section first discusses some trends related to analytic tools, then indulges in some miscellaneous comments about the development of analytic tools for the human factors of end user systems.

RELATED TRENDS

There are three trends that are related to the development of analytic tools: the development of specification languages for interface design, the development of cognitive models of users, and the comparison of formal notations to determine which formalism is easiest to use. I will discuss them very briefly.

Specification Languages

Foley and van Dam [1982] have pointed out that once one has a formal definition, there are two next steps that can be taken. One is to make predictions about user errors, response time, etc, of the kind we have discussed in the section on "analytic tools". The other is to use the definition to drive a simulation of the interface or the actual interface. Foley and van Dam give a number of references to work of this kind which I will not repeat. There appears to be a trend towards development of specification languages to serve this purpose. At the recent conference on Human Factors in Computer Systems at Gaithersburg, Maryland, 1982, an informal special interest group consisting of roughly a dozen people interested in this area was formed. M. Todd, of Tektronix, is serving as the focal point for this group. According to Todd [1982], the "state-of-the-art in the application of formal grammars to user interface specification seems to be largely manual at this point in time". However, he points out that there are tools, such as YACC, for parsing formal grammars and that "the automation of the process may be the next step". If such automation is the next step, however, cognitive information of the kind in the Reisner (SPF) approach will have to be distinguished from the physical input to the system.

A few people interested in specification languages are particularly aiming at improving the human interface. One such example is the work of Bleser and Foley [1982], who have designed a specification language intended both for analysis of human factors and for later mechanization.

User Models

Another trend that is related to the analytic tools discussed in this paper is the development of user models. The term "user model" has two interpretations. It sometimes refers to the model, or image, that the user has about how the system works. Another use of the term is a model, or representation, of the user. Both of these senses of the term are related to the analytic tools in this paper. The CMG of Moran is viewed by him as "a model of the different kinds of knowledge that users have about a system". Kieras and Polson [1982] are describing "users knowledge of how to use [a] device" with a formal grammar, representing the interface formally, and comparing the two representions.

The second sense of the term "user model" (model of the user) is also related to the analytic tools discussed in this paper. The keystroke-level model of Card and Moran and the Reisner Action Language work with SPF are both models in this second sense. They describe the user as a processor, a system that performs certain actions. The notion that thus emerges is that of two processors communicating with each other. The work of Shneiderman [1982], in fact, gives a notation for describing communication for such intercommunicating processors.

Models of the user should include cognitive, or mental operations or actions. The Card and Moran and the Reisner approach take some steps in this direction. This is a crucial step. Cognition is clearly central to ease of use. Of particular importance is the fact that a relationship between cognitive psychology and human factors seems to be taking form. Studies of how the user, as a processor, functions will probably be built into future models and analyses.

Comparison of Notations for Ease of Use

One of the practical requirements for a tool for analysing ease of use is that the tool itself be easy to use. In the discussion of specific analytic tools, discussion of ease of use of the tools was conspicuous by its absence. There is some work, however, in this direction. Specifically, there is interest in determining which of several methods of formal representation is easier to use. An example is the work of Jacob [1982], who compares two formalisms for representing specifications (BNF and state transition diagrams) for comprehensibility.

MISCELLANEOUS DISCUSSION

This section contains a pot-pourri of personal comments on the area of analytic tools for human factors.

What is the State of the Art? It is exciting and gratifying that any work at all is going on in the area of analytic tools for end user systems. Behavioral experimentation to measure ease of use of end user systems, which these tools attempt to augment or replace, is itself very recent. The work on analytic tools is still fairly sparse. It is not well developed. Among the tools that have been specified, only some have been validated. None have been tested for ease of use. It is not yet clear how central to ease of use are the concepts they embody. This is not a criticism of analytic tools. Since the overall space of ease of use problems has not yet been described, even verbally, it is not possible to see how any approach, analytic or otherwise, corresponds to this space. Furthermore, little, if any, thought has been given to which tools should be applied, for which purposes, and at what cost. Such an attempt would clearly be premature in an area which is still groping for basic concepts. However, the fact that the work is being done at all is encouraging.

How do the Keystroke-type Models Differ? The two keystroke models presented are superficially quite similar. However, there is a very subtle, but important, shift of orientation. It is a conjecture of the author that the Embley model had its origin in the kinds of data that can be collected automatically by a system. The model is thus focused on the system, not the user. There is a parameter, T_c in their model. However, this appears to be a catchall parameter which represents both user "think time" and machine response time. It may represent time unaccounted for by an automatic recording system.

The Card and Moran model seems superfically quite similar to the Embley and Nagy model. However, the orientation seems different. With its inclusion of the Mental Operator, the Card and Moran model seems to be truly a model <u>of the user.</u> It is a psychological model.

<u>Why Distinguish the Keystroke and the Language Models?</u> The distinction between keystroke type models and language models merits discussion. These models are in fact related. This can be seen clearly in the Reisner SPF work. Individual "sentences" derived from a grammar in the language models correspond to specific tasks described by the keystroke type models.

Why then do we distinguish the two kinds of models? Because the language models go further. First, the language models include a notion of "structure", and the possibility of difficulty metrics based on this concept. It should be possible to identify specific kinds of inconsistencies in a system using this concept.

Second, the language models offer the potential for "intrinsic" metrics rather than the "task dependent" metrics now available. An intrinsic metric is based on some overall characteristic of the formal description such as the number of rules in a grammar. "Task-dependent metrics" depend on the specific criterion tasks selected for inclusion in a particular analysis. Different results can thus be obtained, depending on the specific tasks selected. It remains to be determined where each kind of metric will be applicable.

Language models also offer a neat way to "package" a description of an entire interaction. Given such packaging, any desired task can be described quickly and easily, on demand, from the grammar. It is possible that such description could be generated automatically. It is not necessary to refer to cumbersome, sometimes incomprehensible and incomplete verbal descriptions. Furthermore, not only can individual tasks be described quickly, but <u>combinations</u> of individual tasks can be described without "flipping pages" to find the relevant action sequences.

<u>Will the Language Models Take Too Long to Create?</u> One question which arises in discussing the language models is: wouldn't it take too long to write a grammar for a large system? The answer is: it probably would take a long time to write a grammar. Would it take too long? That is not clear. It would probably take less time to write a grammar for a system with many functions than to test all of those functions with behavioral tests. It then becomes matter of personal judgement whether any determination of ease of use is feasible in a large system. It is also a matter of personal judgement whether <u>not</u> determining ease of use is worth the potential cost in lost sales and degradation of personal quality of life.

<u>Are the Behavioral and Analytic Approaches in Competition?</u> Behavioral and analytic approaches to human factors are not in competition. In fact, the approaches are complementary and there are clear and necessary interactions between them. Discussion of these interactions would probably fill a book on the philosophy of science. However, a few comments are in order.

Behavioral tests are needed to validate analytic tools and to determine whether or not the tools are easy to use. But validation experiments are more than tests of whether or not a model predicts ease of use correctly. When model and experiment do not agree, there is opportunity for further refinement or development of the model.

Furthermore, behavioral tests provide data on specific parameters that will be used in analytic tools. An example of such data is the work of Farrand [in preparation].

Behavioral experiments can also be the source of analytic tools. For example, they can identify common kinds of errors. Analysis techniques can then attempt to model and predict such errors.

SUMMARY

There is a barely perceptible trend towards development of analytic tools for the human factors of end user systems. The analytic tools are "tools of the trade" for human factors practitioners to use in assessing the ease of use of end user systems. The trend thus falls in the area of methodology development rather than studies of particular end user systems or studies of principles of human factors.

In an "analytic tool" there is: 1) an abstract representation, or model, of the user interface and 2) some method of analysing the representation to predict ease of use. Analytic tools should be validated to determine whether the predictions are correct. They should also be tested for ease of use. This paper gives examples of some analytic tools currently being developed, and comments on the state of the art of their development.

ACKNOWLEDGEMENT

I wish to acknowledge Dr. A. B. Farrand for reading and commenting on this paper, and for many interesting and thoughtful suggestions.

REFERENCES

Bleser, T. & Foley, J. D., Toward specifying and evaluating the human factors of user-computer interfaces, Proc. Human Factors in Computer Systems, Gaithersburg, Md., 1982, 309-314.

Card, S. K. & Moran, T. P., The keystroke-level model for user performance time with interactive systems, Comm. ACM, 1980, 23, 396-410.

Dunsmore, H. E., Using formal grammar as a design tool to predict the most useful characteristics of interactive systems, Office Automation Conference Digest, San Francisco: AFIPS Press, 1982a, 53-56.

Dunsmore, H. E., & Reisner, P., Some further evidence on the formal grammar approach to human factors research, Technical Report 348, Dept. of Computer Sciences, Purdue University, 1982b.

Embley, D. W., Lan, N. T. Leinbaugh, D. W. & Nagy, G., A procedure for predicting program editor performance from the users point of view, Intl. J. of Man-Machine Studies, 1978, 10, 639-650.

Farrand, A. B., Keystrokes and cognition: an experimental comparison, in preparation.

Foley, J. D. & van Dam, A., Fundamentals of Computer Graphics, Reading, MA: Addison-Wesley, 1982.

Jacob, R. J. K., Using formal specification in the design of a human-computer interface, Proc. Human Factors in Computer Systems, Gaithersburg, Md., 1982, 315-321.

Kieras, D. E., & Polson, P. G., An approach to the formal analysis of user complexity, Project on the user complexity of devices and systems, Working Paper No. 2, University of Arizona and University of Colorado, 1982.

Moran, T. P., The command language grammar: a representation for the user interface of interactive computer systems, Intl. J. of Man-Machine Studies, 1981, 15, 3-50.

The Psychology of Human-Computer Interaction, special issue of ACM Computing Surveys, (Moran, T. ed), 1981, 13.

Reisner, P., Formal grammar and human factors design of an interactive graphics system, IEEE Trans. on Software Engineering, 1981a, SE-7, 229-240.

Reisner, P., Human factors studies of database query languages: a survey and assessment, ACM Computing Surveys, 1981b, 13, 13-31.

Reisner, P., Formal grammar as a tool for analyzing ease of use: some fundamental concepts, Human Factors in Computer Systems, (Thomas, J. and Schneider, M. eds), Ablex, in press

Shneiderman, B., Software Psychology, Winthrop, Cambridge, Mass, 1980.

Shneiderman, B., Multiparty grammars and related features for defining interactive systems, IEEE Trans. on Systems, Man and Cybernetics, 1982, SMC-12, 148-154.

Todd, M. personal communication.

Human Factor Aspects in Organizations
and Information Systems Supporting Them

F. Krückeberg
GMD (Gesellschaft für Mathematik und Datenverarbeitung)

St. Augustin/Bonn

Aim

In designing information systems and developing information technology for the future it is desirable to take human factors into account. However the various human factors involved can sometimes be confusing or misleading.

The aim of this paper is to consider these factors systematically, to identify some objectives and the means to achieve them. In this paper more general aspects will be considered rather than procedural details. However, this does not mean that there is little connection with reality. On the contrary, the subject is of considerable practical importance.

Concept

There is a close relationship between Human Factors and Ergonomics. Encyclopaedia Britannica (1965) gives the following definition of Ergonomics: "The study of the relationship between man and his working environment, with special reference to anatomical, physiological and psychological factors". We have to consider here those aspects of Ergonomics relating to information technology.

The Human Factors and ergonomic aspects can be represented by the following matrix:

Level	Human Abilities	Ergonomics
3	Objective-related Abilities (value oriented, integrating and cooperative abilities)	Organizational Ergonomics
2	Cognitive Abilities (Operative thinking)	Communication Ergonomics
1	Sensory Abilites	Technical Ergonomics

In the left column of the matrix Human Abilities are represented systematically at three levels. The Sensory Abilities at level 1 represent the abilities of the sense organs for simple perception, e.g. to see and recognise a graphical symbol. The Cognitive Abilities at level 2 represent the ability to recognise patterns and more complex structures, e.g. to understand a grammatical sentence or to think logically. The Cognitive Abilities are used for example in a dialog at a terminal. It is obvious that the Cognitive Abilities are dependent on the Sensory Abilities. The Objective-related Abilities at level 3 enable man to recognise an objective, to understand a complex task and to use his abilities at the lower levels 2 and 1 for this task. The Objective-related Abilities are value related. They stand for a higher understanding of reality and its values. The Integrating and Cooperative Abilities are closely connected to the Objective-related Abilities. This is because the recognition of objectives and values can or should lead to interest in cooperation and integration of various things or people. For example Managers are expected to have Objective-related Abilities. The higher and more creative an activity is (e.g. with a scientist or top manager), the more important the Objective-related Abilities. The Objective-related Abilities presuppose that Cognitive Abilities exist.

This structure of Human Abilities can also be applied to Ergonomics as represented in the second column of the matrix. At level 1 is Technical Ergonomics. By this is meant for example the arrangement of a visual display terminal (visual display unit, VDU), so that the eyes of the user are not strained. Technical Ergonomics has been found to be of considerable importance in information technology. Discussion of the problems has been lively and controversial so that VDUs have had to be made to exacting specifications. Most of the problems have now been solved so that this paper need not consider them further. It should be noted that in the area of Technical Ergonomics various German standards are being worked out, particularly for VDU work.

Level 2 consists of Communication Ergonomics. It concerns less the configuration of the hardware rather the characteristics of the software. It includes, for example, the structure of a user language, the characteristics of a retrieval structure or the organization of the information available at a VDU. For the same meaning the term Software Ergonomics is used because of its importance for Communication Ergonomics. The term Cognitive Ergonomics is also used as Cognitive Abilities are involved. And so the terminology is not consistent but the meaning is very similar. The term Communication Ergonomics is also used in this paper because of its importance for modern information technology. There is much to do in the field of Communication Ergonomics particularly in the application areas of office automation and conference systems.

Finally level 3 consists of Organizational Ergonomics. This rather new term was first used in a workshop at the IBM Wissenschaftszentrum in Heidelberg in December 1981 by Dzida and the current author. In the meanwhile it has featured at many conferences. Organizational Ergonomics means the activity of adjusting and arranging organization structures for people, with particular emphasis on objectives, values and semantic elements. The support of Cooperative and Integrative Abilities are thereby included. This paper is primarily concerned with Organizational Ergonomics.

If these three levels of Ergonomics are considered together, the following hypothesis can be proposed:

For the ergonomic requirements of a level to be satisfied, the ergonomic requirements of lower levels must have already been satisfied.

This means that there is no point in trying to get the Organizational Ergonomics right unless the Communication Ergonomics are right.

Examples

Examples are now given to show which developments in Information Technology have become desirable because of Organizational Ergonomics.

The support of cooperation within communicative office systems requires an easy way to define cooperating groups and proceedures relevant for a group. Similar requirements apply to conference systems. In this case the cooperation is obvious. As the groups and the forms of cooperation usually change frequently, the reorganisation of such a system should also be easy. Ease of reorganisation of these systems, particularly of communicating office systems, is a requirement which at the moment can hardly be achieved.

Important features of information systems are the method of presentation and the structuring of information. If in accordance with someone's objective-related Abilities information is to be presented so that a part is specially emphasised for his task, then this is a matter for Organizational Ergonomics. The semantic or pragmatic attributes of information could also be presented visually (e.g. highlighting or blinking cursor). Highlighted semantic attributes are particularly helpful for developing the users concept of his task.

Another important function of Organizational Ergonomics is to support role-taking. In interpersonal communication role-taking means to slip into the other person's shoes to understand his or her intentions, objectives and expectations. Role taking is necessary in cooperation procedures, specially in decision making processes. Computer based message and conferencing systems should support role-taking. If such systems do not provide the capabilities for role taking, constructive interpersonal communication is replaced by information distribution along pre-defined path. This limits the individuals potential (= Objective-related Abilities) for adequate problem solving by cooperation. Problems of this type are worked out by the European user Environment subgroup of IFIP WG6.5. A summary- of the intensive activities of this IFIP subgroup is given in the References. The GMD is actively involved in this subgroup.

In this connection reference should be made to experimental tests carried out at the GMD on the GMD conference system KOMEX. Also the research and experimental survey of Müller-Böling has indicated the great importance of flexibility in the working environment for the acceptance by the user of information technology. It can help relations within a cooperative group when the members see the relations in their working environment represented graphically on a VDU.

The most important form of cooperation is a face-to-face conference, well supported before, during and after. And so an important function of information technology is to encourage face-to-face conferences. Information technology should therefore concern itself intensively with the question: How can conference and information systems be organized, so as to improve face-to-face communication and be used it more intensively as a creative, constructive, cooperative and integrating instrument of human work.

Conclusions

Future information technology should take into account not only Technical and Communications Ergonomics but particularly Organizational Ergonomics and use the possibilities of organizational and technical arrangements as required by Organizational Ergonomy. Support and encouragement of face-to-face communication and the creation of cooperative, communicative, integrated forms of working are examples of such arrangements. And so there is a chance to give the user flexibility, which enables him not only to develop his Operative Abilities, but also to apply his ability to cooperate and pursue his objectives. We should therefore develop systems which are flexible and open-ended regarding Human Factors. For the future development of information technology research in Organizational Ergonomics must be pursued vigorously in conjunction with appropriate experimental studies and pilot projects.

Literature

Hiltz, Starr Roxanne; Turoff, Murray:
The Evolution of User Behavior in a Computerized Conferencing System,
Communications of the ACM, Vol. 24, November 1981

Krückeberg, Fritz; Dzida, Wolfgang:
Vortrag über Begriff und Bedeutung der Organisationsergonomie,
IBM Wissenschaftszentrum Heidelberg, Dezember 1981

Kupka, Ingbert; Maass, Susanne; Oberquelle, Horst:
Kommunikation - ein Grundbegriff für die Informatik,
Bericht des Fachbereichs Informatik, Universität Hamburg, 1981

Müller-Böling, Detlef; Müller, Michael:
Zum Zusammenhang zwischen Informationstechnik, Organisationsstruktur und individuellem
Handlungsspielraum,
Arbeitstagung Mensch-Maschine Kommunikation, Bad Honnef 1982

Pankoke-Babatz, Uta, et. al.:
Bericht über die Erfahrungen aus dem KOMEX-Feldtest,
Interner Arbeitsbericht, GMD, August 1982

Reichwald, Ralf; Sorg, Stefan:
Kooperationsbeziehungen in Büro- und Kommunikationstechnik als Managementtechnologie,
Arbeitsbericht aus dem Forschungsschwerpunkt "Personal- und Organisationsforschung unter
besonderer Berücksichtigung technologischer Innovationen",
Hochschule der Bundeswehr, München, 1982

Szyperski, Norbert, et. al.:
Bürosysteme in der Entwicklung,
Friedrich Vieweg u. Sohn, Braunschweig, 1982

Conferences

IFAC/IFIP/IFORS/IEA conference on
"Analysis, Design and Evaluation of Man-Machine Systems"
Baden-Baden, September, 1982

Arbeitstagung Mensch-Maschine Kommunikation
15./16.11.1982, Veranstalter: GMD

Fachtagung "Software-Ergonomie",
28. April 1983, Veranstalter: German Chapter ACM

THE CONTRIBUTION OF ARTIFICIAL INTELLIGENCE
TO THE HUMAN FACTORS OF APPLICATION SOFTWARE

Walther v. Hahn

Research Unit for Information Science
and Artificial Intelligence

University of Hamburg
Mittelweg 179
D-2000 Hamburg 13
Federal Republic of Germany

Summary

This paper deals with some mechanical, cognitive and social aspects of
ergonomy in the following fields of Artificial Intelligence: Vision,
robotics, theorem proving, speech recognition, natural language processing. A few benefits that are now visible are shown. To evaluate the
use of natural language AI-systems, research (1) must consider the natural (language) environment of the problem-solving process with its
heterogeneous types of information, (2) must appreciate highly restricted language utterances as linguistically appropriate to specific task
environments. The benefits of future natural language systems depend
on three conditions:
  - dominance of cognitive and communicative abilities over linguis-
    tic ones,
  - realization of an elementary, dynamic partner model,
  - transparency, as provided by an explanation component.

All attempts to give a precise answer to the question posed in the ti-
tle meet with several difficulties. Let me mention only three of them:

Artificial Intelligence is still in a volatile development phase and
there is nearly no valid criterion to decide wether we are still in the
period of experiments or just at the beginning of a time of widespread
practical use.

Secondly, closely related to the previous statement, it seems to be
most questionable to make inferences about the benefits of Artificial
Intelligence from the claims of those AI-researchers who have never
proven their claims with realistic implementations (e.g. Fifth Generation Program).

Thirdly, for an evaluation of ergonomic aspects of Artificial Intelligence one must inspect AI-systems over a longer period of time and in a variety of situations as well as with a representative number of users of those systems. Such an analysis is not presently available.

Although we must refer to the current state of the art, must rely on perspective statements of AI-insiders, and have no long-term empirical proofs of the benefits of AI-software (with respect to human factors), we hope to present some arguable points for further discussion. Some of the statements are more or less conceptually derived, some are based on empirical data.

Let me first give a rough outline of the aspects of human factors that may be applicable to AI-software products. In a slightly metaphorical way ergonomics have three ranges:

- mechanical ergonomics
  (instrumental optimization, anthropometry, objective
   working conditions, safety, etc.)
- cognitive ergonomics
  (software ergonomics, structuring tools, visualization, adjust-
   ment to decision field, etc.)
- social ergonomics
  (initiative support, cooperation, interaction, subjective
   working conditions, job satisfaction, etc.)

Artificial Intelligence work is being done in the fields shown by figure 1 (cf. NILSSON 1982).

Actual working AI-software in the indicated fields of application provide at least the following benefits in reference to human factors:

Relief from fatiguing observation tasks by scene analysis systems. Those systems at the same time can serve as safe visual-inspection instruments. Visual feedback in tool/machine control as well as in process control can be evaluated automatically. The ergonomic progress concentrates mainly on mechanical ergonomics. A good example may be the checking of electronic chips. When workers at one such working place complained of eye-strain, the task was undertaken by a vision system.

In the field of theorem proving, one may think of inference components of other AI-systems in areas such as medical diagnosis, oil prospection, etc. Especially in knowledge acquisition and knowledge consistency checking Artificial Intelligence techniques can support data base management. This support mainly concerns cognitive ergonomics.

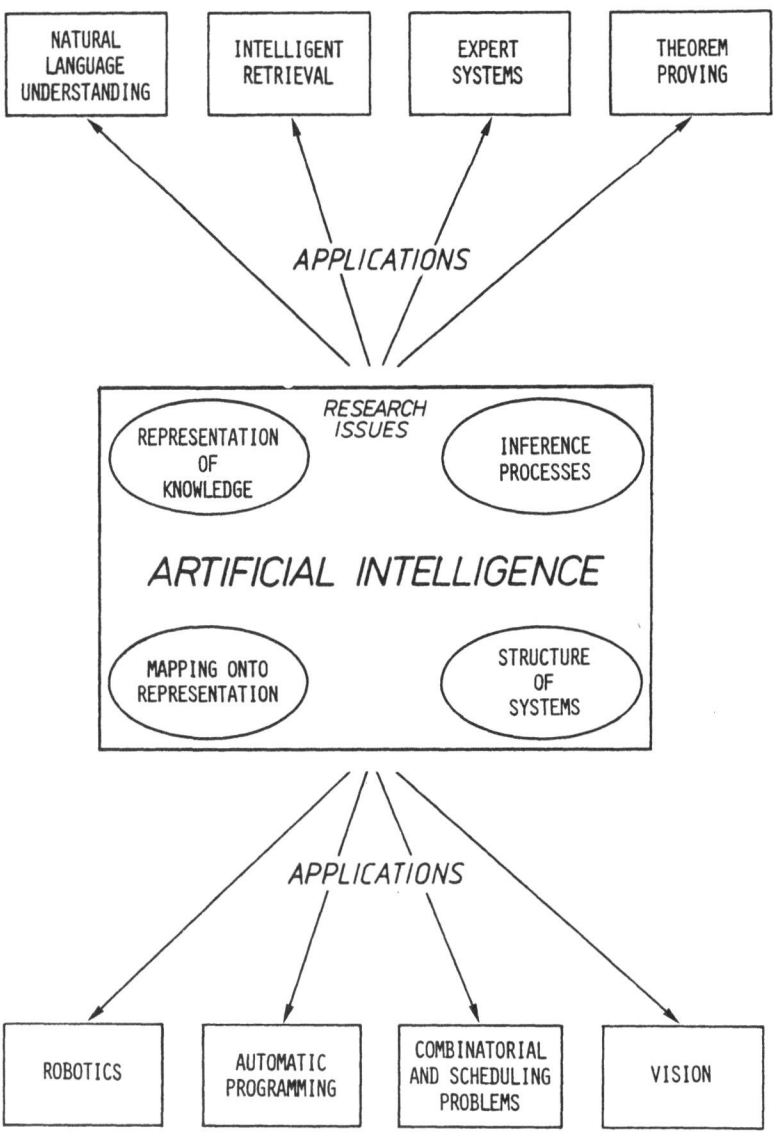

Figure 1: Fields of Artificial Intelligence

In the area of <u>robotics</u>, the ergonomic aspect was the leading one from the beginning of research. Relief from routine tasks and replacing human workers at dangeraus working places have been strong motives for the development of applicable and flexible instruments. Generally, robotics is the most obvious field of ergonomic progress based on AI-techniques.

Speech recognition is not only used in those working stations, in which the worker usually cannot keep his hands free. The subject's hands, which are necessary to transport objects or manipulate control instruments, cannot be used to trigger other information channels in man-machine interaction. The analysis of the spoken word provides the continuous flow of processes on two levels. Moreover, speech recognition, in combination with speech generation, is a very efficient means of integrating handicapped people into the working process. The profit of speech recognition seems to be centered around mechanical ergonomics, but it also has a very strong social component.

Natural language processing is one of the earliest fields of Artificial Intelligence research and at the same time one with a slow rate of progress in terms of application-ready systems. This striking fact is due first to the complexity of natural language syntax, semantics and pragmatics, and secondly to the lack of reliable information about language processes. As a matter of fact, up to now linguists have concentrated on linguistic objects (words, rules, semantics, etc.) rather than on concrete cognitive processes underlying the understanding and generation of natural language. Nevertheless AI techniques have begun to find their way into language transformation software in information science. Abstract-writing systems present information in a condensed form, in a natural language which a user may scan easily. In a broader sense the recent progress in knowledge based machine translation in restricted technical environments can be viewed as having a strong cognitive ergonomic aspect as well.

As far as the ergonomic demand and/or the importance of the task justifies the expense, combined AI-systems (e.g. vision system with natural language access, such as HAM-ANS (cf. MARBURGER etal.1981) may multiply the positive ergonomic effect.

In general, AI-based natural language systems seem to be promising as access systems to other software - for specific users and in cases where high flexibility is needed.

Evidence comes from the business community: The increasing value of informal and imprecise natural language interaction is first of all an issue of recent management research. It was the very application of computers as a source of rapidly-obtainable 'hard' organizational data that showed that mere uninterpreted hard data about a firm only allow planning by extrapolation (cf. LUCAS 1975). All other information about innovations by means of prognoses, trend observation, etc. is by na-

ture 'soft' natural language information (inquiries, beliefs, ratings)
summarized afterwards by applying condensing techniques. Every efficient
use of this condensed information is based on knowledge about the original pragmatic and linguistic context (see figure 2).

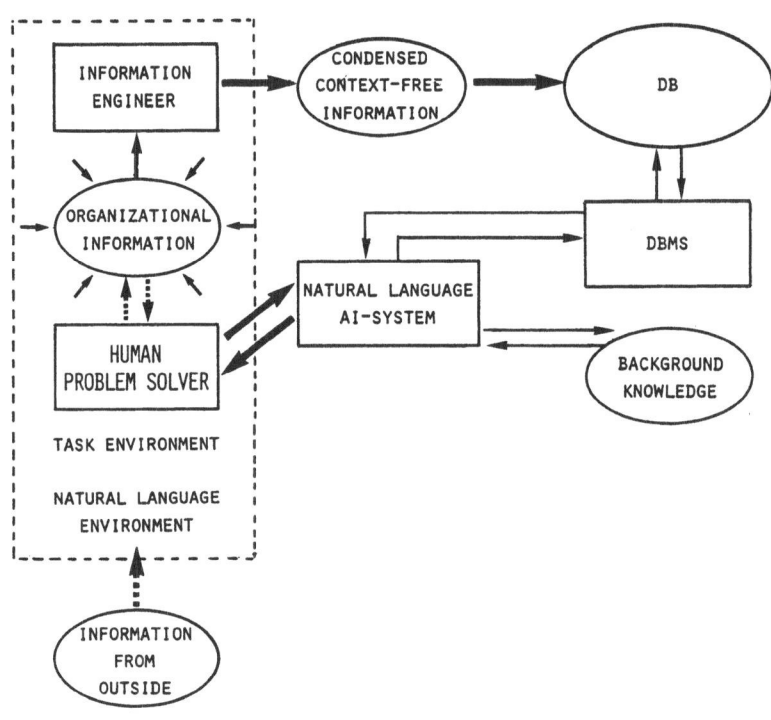

Figure 2 : Natural language access to condensed data

BARTRAM (1969) indicates four main types of formal communication in an
organization (the following are English translations of the names given
to these processes by BARTRAM in German):

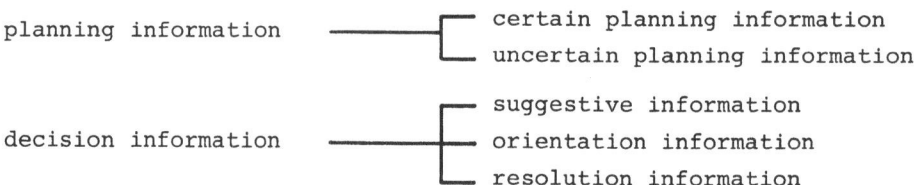

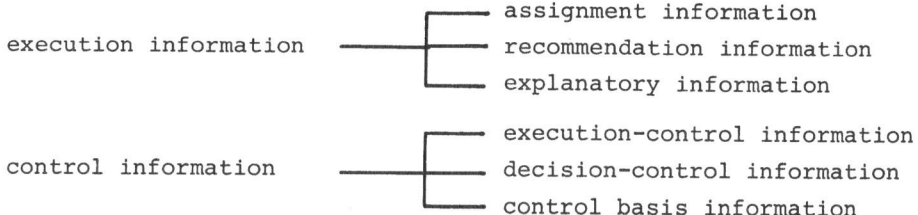

It is quite obvious, that some information, particularly suggestive information or explanatory information will not be available as numerical data or even in a form that is directly appropriate to decision-making, but as natural language statements in discussions, brainstorming sessions, interpretative remarks, etc.

Even though up to now these fuzzy types of information can be handled by man-machine communication systems (cf. WAHLSTER 1981) only to a small degree, the future user or customer of integrated information systems will obviously desire natural language access to all types of information systems (not restricted to data bases available today).

As MORIK (1983) shows, their requirements are, among others: better substanciated decision (64,9%), better control in computer interaction (71,1%), more transparency (65,2%). This result of a general inquiry among 927 firms was complemented by personel interviews with experts from leading computer firms, consulting firms and software producers. A further interesting detail of the inquiry was that, in the opinion of 59,3% of the interviewees, natural language interaction should be strongly bound to concrete actions of a system according to the outcome of the dialogue (e.g. writing forms, bills, performing scheduling tasks).

Theoretical management requirements and real inquiry data show that the deeper one integrates complex information processes in a system, the more natural language seems to be an appropriate tool for organizing man-machine interaction.

The word 'tool' however, might be misleading. A natural language component cannot be implemented as an independent module containing linguistic rules and lexicon entries. Language is embedded in a set of cognitive abilities of which natural language often is only the indication. Therefore it is useless merely to verbalize expressions of a formal data base query language, because every casual user will interpret this utterance according to his natural language experience with human partners. For most frequent users, on the other hand, communication in a formal language in this case will be more efficient, provided that the data base contains only context-independent 'hard' data. Otherwise the information process must be more deeply integrated into the problem-solving environment.

What is meant by deeper integration? Only a small class of information-seeking processes either concern precise objective facts or are limited to single turns taken by the dialogue partner. Most human information prosesses are performed by a sequence of coherent requests at different levels: methodical, factual, pragmatic.

The following hypothetical examples show some of these features. Details of the implementation in HAM-ANS being under work are contained in MARBURGER/NEBEL (1982). The data base deals with fishing voyages (ca. 11 MByte, access via PASCAL/R).   (U = user; S = system)

U: What's the difference between the ships 'Oceanus' and 'Otto Hahn'?
S: The 'Otto Hahn' has (...).

The system needs additional background knowledge, which is neither contained nor even representable in the data base.

U: Which ships have cruised in the same area?
S: (A) and (B).

The system needs imlicit information in the data base, which must be inferred from definite statements. Certainly the two ships did not cruise over exactly the same points. The corresponding expression of PASCAL/R is:

```
➤ Var ships: relation <S1,S2> of record S1:
  shipname; S2:shipname end;

➤ ships[<c.vessel-nam,c1.vessel-nam>of
  each c in cruises, each c1 in cruises:
  ((((c.box-lat-n >c1.box-lat-n) and
  (c.box-lat-s <c1.box-lat-s)) and (((
  c.box-long-w >c1.box-long-w) and (
  c.box-long-e <c1.box-long-w)) or ((
  c.box-long-w >c1.box-long-e) and (
  c.box-long-e <c1.box-long-e))) and
  (c.vessel-nam ◇ c1.vessel-nam)))] ;
  ➤ships;
```

U: Which ships came from Athens?
S: (C) and (D).
U: Which of these is driven by nuclear power?
S: (C).

The system performs coherent evaluation by focussing on stored interim results.

U: How long will the answer take?

S: (x) minutes.

U: Then stop the evaluation!

This is a pragmatic meta-question at the processing level.

The above shown information seeking behaviour is typical of sessions with casual users and very large data bases. Comparisons with PASCAL/R and the same data base showed that it is difficult to acquire enough information without natural language.

On the other hand, a closer look at natural language in working environment leads to the realization that natural language consists of a broad variety of styles. A homogeneous style of technical language seems to be an inadmissable idealized notion. Studies in technical languages (cf. KITTREDGE/LEHRBERGER (1982), v.HAHN (1983)) demonstrate, that variations in performance depend on the specifications of at least three dimensions in every communication situation:

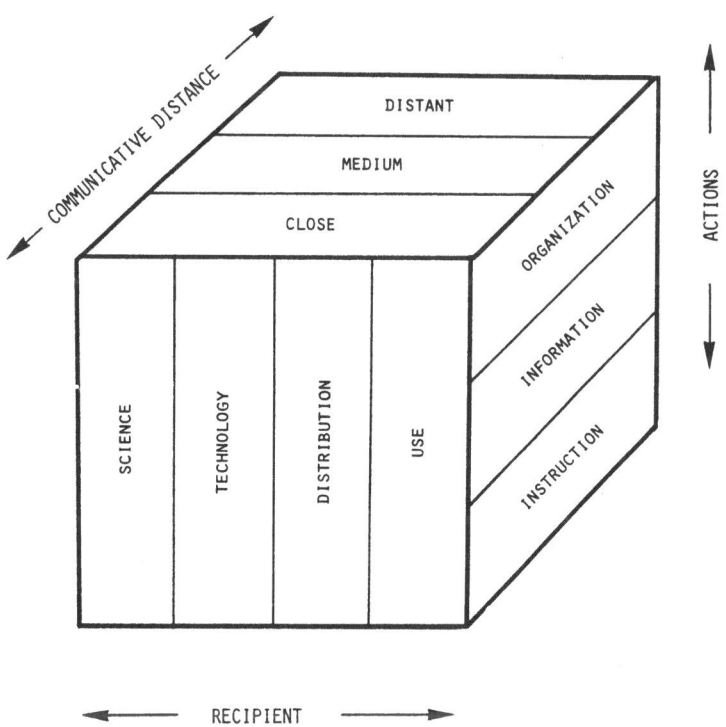

Figure 3: Dimensions of technical language

According to the actual specification of the communicative distance, the type of action and the recipient, the structure of the language performance will vary from extremely shortened forms (comparable to menues) or extremely formalized utterances (you may remember the 'mark twain' on Mississippi steamboats), up to unrestricted, spontaneous and individual talk.

So, it cannot be the overall goal of natural language interfaces to provide some sort of essayistic communication independent of the performed task, the recipient and the (organizational) shared knowledge of the partners.

In former periods of history specific styles of natural language were even developed according to new ways of communication, as the telegraphic style.

Correspondingly, psychological research provides evidence (FLAMMER (1981) of the high predictability of the questions people ask in well-defined and task-oriented situations (the description of a car accident). They propose a special text grammar mechanism, which to a certain degree even predicts the sequence of the questions. They also show that shared knowledge about a well-structured situation is necessary. In any other cases it is necessary for the dialogue participants to communicate explicitly about

- the minimal starting information of the asking partner
- the specific goal
- his/her wish to ask at all
- his/her timing of the questions
- his/her conviction that the partner is willing to give
  information and is able to do so.

In other words a system either works in a standardized pragmatic situation or performs at least a minimum of meta-communication to build up a partner's model from which, combined with stereotyped knowledge, specific predictions can be derived.

In the last two sections we stated that efficient support of human information processing includes a deeper integration of a coherent sequence of actions, but on the other hand implies the performance of task specific linguistic methods of communication. Artificial Intelligence already meets some of the above-mentioned requirements even in realistic applications, others seem to be within reach.

A remarkable progress of natural language systems and their ergonomic benefits could now only be achieved with the fulfillment of three basic conditions (cf. WAHLSTER/v.HAHN (1981)):

(1) The dominance of communicative and cognitive abilities over natural language performance must be obtained.

Natural language utterances and all parts of them (such as semantics, presuppositions) must be seen as clear indicators of correspondingly performed cognitive abilities. Since any user, particularly the novice or casual user, of natural language systems will associate its perform-ance with that of a human partner, a superficial simulation of natural language is misleading and inefficient. Therefore most of the work to be done in natural language systems should concentrate on conceptual, semantic and pragmatic abilities and not on attractive stylistics. Of special importance in this field will be focus recognition, pragmatical-ly based ellipses analysis and generation, and speech act recognition.

(2) Every really flexible system must at least contain an elementary dynamic partner model, which covers more than a static list of user classes.

Even if the system does not update the contents of the partner model by analysing presuppositions or implicit beliefs, it must keep track of the mutual knowledge and adapt elementary discourse strategies according to the degree of comprehensiveness desired by the user.

(3) Every really transparent system must contain an explanation compo-nent which reacts on both levels, the factual and the methodological one.

The system must be able to give both explanations concerning inferences and reasons concerning facts. The individual responsibility of the user for his/her decisions is only guaranteed if the user can evaluate the answer given by the system. Otherwise a user has no basis on which to decide whether or not to believe and accept the systems answer.

References:

BARTRAM, P., Die betriebliche Kommunikation. Frankfurt/M. 1969

FLAMMER, A. et al., Predicting what Questions People Ask. In: Psycho-logical Research 43 (1981), 421-429

v.HAHN, W., Deutsche Fachsprachen. Berlin 1983

v.HAHN, W., Überlegungen zum Handlungsrahmen von Fragen in Artificial-Intelligence-Systemen. In: Krallmann, D./STICKEL, G.(eds.), Zur Theorie der Frage. Tübingen 1981, 185-191

HOEPPNER, W./JAMESON, A., Kooperatives Dialogverhalten im Simulations-
        system HAM-RPM. In: Proceedings of 4th workshop on Arti-
        ficial Intelligence. Bad Honnef 1979, 21-31

KITTREDGE, R./LEHRBERGER, J.(eds.), Sublanguage. Studies of Language
        in Restricted Semantic Domains. Berlin/New York 1982

LUCAS, H.C., Why Information Systems Fail. New York/London 1975

MARBURGER, H./NEUMANN, B./NOVAK, H.-J., Natural Language Dialogue
        about Moving Objects in Automatically analyzed traffic
        scenes. In: Proceedings of 7th Int. Conference on
        Artificial Intelligence, Vancouver 1981, 49-51

MORIK, K., Demand and Requirements for Natural Language Systems -
        Results of an Inquiry.Jan. 1983. (Research Unit for Infor-
        mation Science and Artificial Intelligence, University of
        Hamburg, Report Nr. 14). Paper submitted for IJCAI 1983

NEBEL, B./MARBURGER,H., Das natürlichsprachliche System HAM-ANS:
        Intelligenter Zugriff auf heterogene Wissens- und Daten-
        basen. In: Proceedings of GI 12. Jahrestagung. Berlin/
        New York 1982

NILSSON, Nils J., Principles of Artificial Intelligence. Berlin/
        New York 1982

TODD, J., Management Control Systems: A Key Link between Strategy,
        Structure and Employee. In: Organzational Dynamics 1977,1
        65-78

WAHLSTER, W., Implementing Fuzziness in Dialogue Systems. In: Rieger,
        B.B.(ed.), Empirical Semantics. Bochum 1981, Vol.I, 259-280

WAHLSTER, W./v.HAHN, W., Mensch-Maschine-Kommunikation auf der Basis
        natürlicher Sprache. (Research Unit for Information Science
        and Artificial Intelligence, University of Hamburg, Memo
        GEN-2) Oct. 1981

Vol. 107: International Colloquium on Formalization of Programming Concepts. Proceedings. Edited by J. Diaz and I. Ramos. VII, 478 pages. 1981.

Vol. 108: Graph Theory and Algorithms. Edited by N. Saito and T. Nishizeki. VI, 216 pages. 1981.

Vol. 109: Digital Image Processing Systems. Edited by L. Bolc and Zenon Kulpa. V, 353 pages. 1981.

Vol. 110: W. Dehning, H. Essig, S. Maass, The Adaptation of Virtual Man-Computer Interfaces to User Requirements in Dialogs. X, 142 pages. 1981.

Vol. 111: CONPAR 81. Edited by W. Händler. XI, 508 pages. 1981.

Vol. 112: CAAP '81. Proceedings. Edited by G. Astesiano and C. Böhm. VI, 364 pages. 1981.

Vol. 113: E.-E. Doberkat, Stochastic Automata: Stability, Nondeterminism, and Prediction. IX, 135 pages. 1981.

Vol. 114: B. Liskov, CLU, Reference Manual. VIII, 190 pages. 1981.

Vol. 115: Automata, Languages and Programming. Edited by S. Even and O. Kariv. VIII, 552 pages. 1981.

Vol. 116: M. A. Casanova, The Concurrency Control Problem for Database Systems. VII, 175 pages. 1981.

Vol. 117: Fundamentals of Computation Theory. Proceedings, 1981. Edited by F. Gécseg. XI, 471 pages. 1981.

Vol. 118: Mathematical Foundations of Computer Science 1981. Proceedings, 1981. Edited by J. Gruska and M. Chytil. XI, 589 pages. 1981.

Vol. 119: G. Hirst, Anaphora in Natural Language Understanding: A Survey. XIII, 128 pages. 1981.

Vol. 120: L. B. Rall, Automatic Differentiation: Techniques and Applications. VIII, 165 pages. 1981.

Vol. 121: Z. Zlatev, J. Wasniewski, and K. Schaumburg, Y12M Solution of Large and Sparse Systems of Linear Algebraic Equations. IX, 128 pages. 1981.

Vol. 122: Algorithms in Modern Mathematics and Computer Science. Proceedings, 1979. Edited by A. P. Ershov and D. E. Knuth. XI, 487 pages. 1981.

Vol. 123: Trends in Information Processing Systems. Proceedings, 1981. Edited by A. J. W. Duijvestijn and P. C. Lockemann. XI, 349 pages. 1981.

Vol. 124: W. Polak, Compiler Specification and Verification. XIII, 269 pages. 1981.

Vol. 125: Logic of Programs. Proceedings, 1979. Edited by E. Engeler. V, 245 pages. 1981.

Vol. 126: Microcomputer System Design. Proceedings, 1981. Edited by M. J. Flynn, N. R. Harris, and D. P. McCarthy. VII, 397 pages. 1982.

Voll. 127: Y. Wallach, Alternating Sequential/Parallel Processing. X, 329 pages. 1982.

Vol. 128: P. Branquart, G. Louis, P. Wodon, An Analytical Description of CHILL, the CCITT High Level Language. VI, 277 pages. 1982.

Vol. 129: B. T. Hailpern, Verifying Concurrent Processes Using Temporal Logic. VIII, 208 pages. 1982.

Vol. 130: R. Goldblatt, Axiomatising the Logic of Computer Programming. XI, 304 pages. 1982.

Vol. 131: Logics of Programs. Proceedings, 1981. Edited by D. Kozen. VI, 429 pages. 1982.

Vol. 132: Data Base Design Techniques I: Requirements and Logical Structures. Proceedings, 1978. Edited by S.B. Yao, S.B. Navathe, J.L. Weldon, and T.L. Kunii. V, 227 pages. 1982.

Vol. 133: Data Base Design Techniques II: Proceedings, 1979. Edited by S.B. Yao and T.L. Kunii. V, 229–399 pages. 1982.

Vol. 134: Program Specification. Proceedings, 1981. Edited by J. Staunstrup. IV, 426 pages. 1982.

Vol. 135: R.L. Constable, S.D. Johnson, and C.D. Eichenlaub, An Introduction to the PL/CV2 Programming Logic. X, 292 pages. 1982.

Vol. 136: Ch. M. Hoffmann, Group-Theoretic Algorithms and Graph Isomorphism. VIII, 311 pages. 1982.

Vol. 137: International Symposium on Programming. Proceedings, 1982. Edited by M. Dezani-Ciancaglini and M. Montanari. VI, 406 pages. 1982.

Vol. 138: 6th Conference on Automated Deduction. Proceedings. 1982. Edited by D.W. Loveland. VII, 389 pages. 1982.

Vol. 139: J. Uhl, S. Drossopoulou, G. Persch, G. Goos, M. Dausmann, G. Winterstein, W. Kirchgässner, An Attribute Grammar for the Semantic Analysis of Ada. IX, 511 pages. 1982.

Vol. 140: Automata, Languages and programming. Edited by M. Nielsen and E.M. Schmidt. VII, 614 pages. 1982.

Vol. 141: U. Kastens, B. Hutt, E. Zimmermann, GAG: A Practical Compiler Generator. IV, 156 pages. 1982.

Vol. 142: Problems and Methodologies in Mathematical Software Production. Proceedings, 1980. Edited by P.C. Messina and A. Murli. VII, 271 pages. 1982.

Vol. 143: Operating Systems Engineering. Proceedings, 1980. Edited by M. Maekawa and L.A. Belady. VII, 465 pages. 1982.

Vol. 144: Computer Algebra. Proceedings, 1982. Edited by J. Calmet. XIV, 301 pages. 1982.

Vol. 145: Theoretical Computer Science. Proceedings, 1983. Edited by A.B. Cremers and H.P. Kriegel. X, 367 pages. 1982.

Vol. 146: Research and Development in Information Retrieval. Proceedings, 1982. Edited by G. Salton and H.-J. Schneider. IX, 311 pages. 1983.

Vol. 147: RIMS Symposia on Software Science and Engineering. Proceedings, 1982. Edited by E. Goto, I. Nakata, K. Furukawa, R. Nakajima, and A. Yonezawa. V. 232 pages. 1983.

Vol. 148: Logics of Programs and Their Applications. Proceedings, 1980. Edited by A. Salwicki. VI, 324 pages. 1983.

Vol. 149: Cryptography. Proceedings, 1982. Edited by T. Beth. VIII, 402 pages. 1983.

Vol. 150: Enduser Systems and Their Human Factors. Proceedings, 1983. Edited by A. Blaser and M. Zoeppritz. III, 138 pages. 1983.